# How to

# Say NO

# Without

# Feeling

# Guilty

# How to Say NO Without Feeling Guilty

*And Say YES to More Time, More Joy, and What Matters Most to You*

Patti Breitman and Connie Hatch

BROADWAY BOOKS

New York

Visit our Web site at www.broadwaybooks.com

Library of Congress Cataloging-in-Publication Data

Breitman, Patti.
How to say no without feeling guilty: and say yes to more time, more
joy, and what matters most to you / by Patti Breitman and Connie
Hatch—1st ed.
    p.   cm.
Includes index.
1. Assertiveness (Psychology)   2. Interpersonal communication.
I. Hatch, Connie.   II. Title.
BF575.A85 B74 2000
158.2—dc21                                          99-048189
                                                         CIP

FIRST EDITION

ISBN 0-7679-0379-X

00   01   02   03   04   10   9   8   7   6   5   4   3   2

*To Stan and Fran, with*

*gratitude and love*

—P B

*To Joey, with love*

*and in memory of*

*Kathryn and Ray Hatch,*

*who said no wisely and well*

*(but not too much)*

—C H

# Acknowledgments

For their professional expertise and commitment to this project, the authors would like to thank all the talented, hardworking people at Broadway Books, especially Steve Rubin, Bob Asahina, Gerry Howard, Robert Allen, Debbie Stier, Catherine Pollock, Roberto de Vicq de Cumptich, Stanley Cohen, and the terrific sales reps. We are particularly indebted to our perceptive and immensely skilled editors, Tracy Behar and Angela Casey. Thanks are also due to Maureen Sugden for her helpful suggestions.

For his early and enthusiastic belief in this book, Bill Shinker

For his wisdom, kindness, and for writing such a generous foreword, Richard Carlson

For her unsurpassed international know-how and incomparable style, Linda Michaels, and for their continual expert help, Teresa Cavanaugh, Helene Blatny, Martha Di Domenico, Eva Betzwieser, and Jenny Thor

For her boundless energy, imagination and PR savvy, Rita Marcus

For helping us in our research, Claude Palmer and Open Secret Bookstore, Shereen Ash at the Fairfax Library, and Kathleen O'Neill

For sharing so much of their time, wisdom, and professional

expertise, we are enormously grateful to Deborah Carroll, Paula Solomon, and Linda Wade

For their valuable insights and feedback, which contributed so much to this book, Lori Baird, Corinda Carford, Tom Cavalieri, Jodi Conway, Joanna Dales, Maggie Gelosi, Valerie Green, Peter Greene, Aron Hirt-Manheimer, Ana Jawerbaum, Edith Joyce, Susan Joyce, Barbara Kops, Renee Martin, Dan Neuharth, Mary Rae, Rose Rawlings, Bob Rosenfeld, David Rosenfeld, Nancy Samalin, Patrice Serret, Evelyn Schmidt, Diane Schube, Lana Staheli, Sandra Stahman, and Donna Starito

In addition, Patti would like to thank:

For her great love and constant belief in me, Fran Zitner

For teaching me about the Golden Rule and for being the most steadfast and best friend, role model, and cheerleader anyone could hope to have, Debby Drezon

For their friendship and enormous help in my office and my life, Dominique Blanchard and Lisa T. Lewis

For her terrific public-speaking advice and generous spirit, Susan Harrow

For their ongoing friendship, Linda Rosinsky, Marion L. Musante, and Josephine Codoni Leary Burke

For their inspiring work on behalf of the planet and its inhabitants, and for calling attention to countless important causes that cry out for a resounding yes, Carol Adams, Neal Barnard, Freyah Dinshah, Jay Dinshah, Gail Davis, Suzanne Havala, Ruth Heidrich, Michael Klaper, James Michael Lennon,

Howard Lyman, Glen Merzer, Mark Messina, Virginia Messina, Victoria Moran, Marr Nealon, Ingrid Newkirk, Carol Normandi, Jennifer Raymond, Laurelee Roark, John Robbins, Robert David Roth, Timothy Smith, Charles Stahler, Deborah Wasserman, and Ann and Larry Wheat

For their persistent support and wisdom in words and silence, motion and stillness, Anna Douglas, Terry Vandiver, and the wonderful women and men in the Friday morning Spirit Rock sangha

And most of all, for his forbearance while this book was a priority, his excellent feedback and input, his computer support, terrific sense of humor, abiding love, and too many gifts to name, Stan Rosenfeld, to whom I'm glad I said yes


Connie would also like to acknowledge:

For their enduring loyalty and encouragement, and for being there all these years: Ken Hatch, Doug Trazzare, Sandi Trazzare, Richard O'Connor, and Deborah Schorsch

Special thanks to my husband and best pal, Joey Cavalieri, for his superheroic support while this book was being written

## The Art of Disappearing

When they say Don't I know you?
say no.

When they invite you to the party
remember what parties are like
before answering.
Someone telling you in a loud voice
they once wrote a poem.
Greasy sausage balls on a paper plate.
Then reply.

If they say We should get together
say why?

It's not that you don't love them anymore.
You're trying to remember something
too important to forget.
Trees. The monastery bell at twilight.
Tell them you have a new project.
It will never be finished.

When someone recognizes you in a grocery
   store
nod briefly and become a cabbage.
When someone you haven't seen in ten years
appears at the door,
don't start singing him all your new songs.
You will never catch up.

Walk around feeling like a leaf.
Know you could tumble any second.
*Then* decide what to do with your time.

— NAOMI SHIHAB NYE

# Contents

# Foreword

by Richard Carlson

..................................................................

*How to Say No Without Feeling Guilty* is a book I desperately needed to read. And boy, am I glad I did. It's one of the most practical and helpful books I've ever read. By implementing only a tiny fraction of the suggestions, I have saved far more time than the time it took to read them. Even before I finished reading the book, I was reaping its rewards. How's that for quick results?

By learning to say no without feeling guilty, you will find time you never dreamed you had. Even more important, you will learn to say yes to all those things that you hold most dear to your heart, things that you really want to do but never seem to have the time for because you're so busy doing other things, saying yes, and filling up your life with commitments and obligations you wish would go away. When you learn to say no, your life will be yours again. Rather than being last on your own priority list, you will emerge as the captain of your own ship, able to make decisions from a place of passion, wisdom, and confidence, rather than out of guilt, fear, or a feeling of being manipulated.

There's no question that for most of us, life has become complicated, if not completely frenetic. Our schedules are bursting at the seams, and frustration is rampant. It would seem that technology and timesaving gadgets should solve our problems, but in most  cases they don't. Sure, we save time with new devices, but because we aren't able to say no, we simply fill up the time we save by saying yes to even more requests. Sadly, we often end up with even tighter schedules and more frustration. We wonder how we are going to prioritize and get it all done.

Learning to say no without guilt can solve this problem. It is interesting to consider that a single, appropriate, and heartfelt "no" can save you more time than even the most sophisticated technology. How many times have you taken on too much—personally or professionally—by saying yes? How many decisions have you made out of guilt or obligation rather than out of love? How often have you committed to some time-consuming task that, in retrospect, you realized you never wanted to take on and perhaps didn't have to do? What if you had been able to say no to at least a portion of these things? What if you had saved your "yeses" for the things that really matter? What would your life be like if you lived it the way you really wanted to?

For a long time I felt, as many do, that learning to say no might be a selfish thing to do. I was wrong. Learning to say no to those unappealing or unreasonable requests—and doing so without guilt—is one of the best ways to become less selfish. What I've discovered is that when I make decisions not from guilt but from my heart, I feel emotionally fulfilled and in harmony with myself. I'm sure you will agree that whenever you have what you need emotionally, your natural instinct will be to reach out to others in compassionate, generous, and loving ways.

I can assure you that as I've learned to say no to certain things and requests, I've been far more available, effective, compassionate, energetic, and generous to the people, organizations, and causes that are dear to me. Both my life and the world around me are better off because I have learned to say no.

To see how this works, think of what it's like when your emotional needs aren't being met—when you feel that your life isn't your own, when you're feeling resentful, as if you never have any time for yourself. It is difficult to spend energy on others, let alone with gentleness or with kindness when you are feeling predominantly overwhelmed.

Another fear I had about saying no was that I felt I would end up hurting too many feelings along the way. I was wrong again! I've found, as the authors of this book point out, that most people have enormous respect for those who make decisions not from guilt but from loving and firm convictions. I have discovered that I can say no to virtually any request in a way that the other person truly understands. Looking back, it is clear that I hurt far more feelings with my lack of conviction, made-up excuses, and wishy-washy decision-making skills than I have since learning to say no without guilt.

I know that this book is about learning to say no, but to this book I say yes, yes, yes! I send my gratitude and best wishes to the authors, and thank them for helping me to help myself. I know that you, too, can learn to say no without feeling guilty, so that you can say yes to whatever matters most in your life.

Treasure yourself.

—Richard Carlson, Ph.D., author of
*Don't Sweat the Small Stuff . . . and It's All Small Stuff*

# Introduction
# The Power of No

It's a short, simple word. Not hard to pronounce. So why is "no" sometimes the hardest word to get out of our mouths? Because "no" is also a very powerful word. And like any powerful thing, it can help us or hurt us.

Consider the power you exercise just by saying the word "no." It can get you out of that lunch date you really don't want to make. It can keep people from taking up your valuable time. It can tell someone who asks for too many favors that it's time to stop taking advantage of you. It can save you money. "No" is an indispensable tool that helps preserve your time and energy for the things that are important to you.

But because it's such a powerful tool, "no" can also be dangerous, and must be used with skill. It can disappoint people you care about, hurt their feelings, or make them angry. Every time you decline an invitation or turn down someone's request, you risk stirring up unpleasantness or conflict. When that happens, it can leave you feeling terribly guilty. *(Uh-oh, I've really ticked her off now. If only I'd agreed to go to her Amway recruitment meeting, everything would have been fine. I was just going to spend time alone at home anyway. I really had no good reason for not going. . . .)*

Women, who traditionally take on more responsibility for relationships, seem to have an especially hard time saying no. We tend to assume it's our job to make sure everybody else is happy. So we go out of our way to be accommodating, even if it means agreeing to make the potato salad when we're already in charge of the charcoal, ice, and beach umbrellas.

As much as we hate rejection, we also hate reject*ing*. Faced with a potentially guilt-inducing situation, it's easier to take the path of least resistance. While inside we may be screaming, "No! Go away! Leave me alone!" on the outside we summon up an agreeable smile and utter that fateful "Okay!"

## Why You Need to Say No

So what's wrong with being accommodating? Not a thing. It's very satisfying to offer support to the people we love, help out a neighbor, or do something positive for the community. Knowing that we're making a difference in someone's life is a great feeling.

The conflict arises when we continually agree to things that please everyone but ourselves or when we commit to tasks for which we have no time or desire.

Family members deserve our love and emotional support, but not every last ounce of our time and energy. We may have to work for a living, but we don't have to be exploited, undervalued, or degraded. People trying to sell us things have no right to pressure us into buying what we don't want—even if they happen to be our good friends.

Day-to-day life is full of questions that provoke a resounding desire to say no. But too often we shrink from using the power of "no" when we should be embracing it. Out of guilt or fear of confrontation, we take on more projects, invest in someone else's priorities, or agree to attend parties we know we'll hate. In the process, we dissipate our most valuable personal resources—time, energy, and money—on things that aren't important to us. Each time we agree to something without enthusiasm or interest, we waste a little more of these precious resources.

## What's So Great About Being Busy?

Not too long ago, when someone asked, "How are you?" the customary response was "Fine, thanks, and you?" But as Richard Carlson points out in his book *Don't Sweat the Small Stuff with Your Family*, a new response has developed to this question. Today when asked "How are you?" the typical person answers, "Busy." Being fine just isn't enough anymore.

It has become almost a cliché in our culture to say that we're stressed out. This leaner, post-downsized era sees many of us working longer hours with less support on the job. For parents, there's the ongoing quest for more family time and the compelling need to stay close to the kids in an increasingly complex and threatening world. As the backdrop for our speeded-up lives, we're subject to information overload and nonstop commercial assaults from morning till night. Every day we are confronted by forces—some serious, some petty—that eat up our time, deplete our resources, and add noise and clutter to our lives.

We feel put-upon and oppressed because it seems there's never enough time for the things we *really* want to do. We go through our busy routines—work, school, kids, household obligations, outside commitments—and wonder why life feels so unsatisfying.

There are hundreds of good books we can turn to for advice on how to manage our time better, get more organized, and set up all kinds of systems at home and on the job. Women's magazines are very happy to tell us how to hurry up and do things faster: *Get dressed in five minutes. Do your hair and makeup in ten minutes. Make dinner in fifteen minutes.*

But there *is* another way of coping with all this busy-ness. Instead of revving up our lives to cram in more, we can also slow down and eliminate some of the clutter and clatter. This book is based on the assumption that by developing the art of saying no, we can cut down on the unsatisfying busy-ness in our lives, in turn creating the time and space for more fulfilling pursuits.

## How to Ruin Relationships: Agree to Everything

. . . . . . . . . . . . . . . . . . . . . . . . . . . . . . . . . . . . . . . . .

When we fall into the habit of "yes-ing" to avoid conflict, we're not really solving anything—we're just trading in one problem for another. The consequences of caving in again and again are likely to be more serious and enduring than any distress resulting from an artfully delivered "no."

Say your brother asks you to help him paint his house on Saturday. If you've got no plans, and you like working outdoors and spending time with your brother—great! On the other hand, if you had your heart set on going sailing, and the smell of paint makes you dizzy, and your brother gets on your nerves anyway—that's a different story. You're going to have a lousy time—and resent your brother even more for ruining your weekend.

Now imagine how you'd feel if this type of scenario played itself out on a regular basis. Maybe you'd try to bury your anger, only to have it seep out gradually in bitter, cranky remarks. Or you may turn it all inward, feeling powerless, possibly even becoming depressed. Eventually you might get fed up and have a big fight. If you're always letting others take advantage of your good nature, that good nature can turn bad pretty quickly.

It's even worse when you're so invested in being "nice" that you say yes to things and then follow through on them badly, halfheartedly, or not at all. By promising something you can't deliver, you set a big trap for yourself and then walk right into it. The irony is that while trying so hard to please, you can end up looking careless, thoughtless, inept, or irresponsible.

But beyond the damage it can do to relationships, "going along" all the time creates practical problems that affect your everyday life in visible, measurable ways. When you accept an unwelcome invitation or commit your time to a project you don't care about, you leave yourself less time for the things you _do_ care about—whether it's playing with your kids, relaxing with your spouse, practicing the guitar, hiking up a mountain, or volunteering at a crisis hotline. The flip side of saying no without guilt—the "yes" side—is about identifying and nurturing the people, causes, and spiritual connections that have meaning for you. And the more vivid your image of what you want to say yes to, the easier it becomes to say no to all that distracts you from your path.

It's not only a question of pleasing yourself. Suppose one of your co-workers asks you to contribute to her favorite charitable organization. Few of us would want to refuse such a request, and if you believe in the cause and can spare the donation—no problem. However, there may be times when you'd prefer not to contribute. The reasons could be philosophical, financial, or something else entirely. So what do you do? Should you support a cause you don't believe in? Or part with money you'd earmarked for a cause that's important to *you*?

## You *Can* Say No and Be Nice

There is a way to decline requests like this—and it doesn't involve turning yourself into a cold, heartless beast. You *can* learn to use the word "no" with skill and sensitivity. This book will provide you with the techniques and phrases to help you say no like a master in a wide variety of real-life situations. It will help you set limits when people are encroaching on you and establish more control over those areas of your life that are being eroded by unwanted requests, information overload, and the endless impositions of modern life.

In the chapters that follow, you will find out how to handle unreasonable demands on the job and how to say no diplomatically to family and friends. We'll suggest ways of responding to appeals for money and ways of removing that nagging sense of guilt through a life approach that emphasizes generosity in a broader context. You'll even find effective ways to say no to commercial transactions and fend off telemarketers and junk mail for good.

## The Joy of Yes

Ultimately, saying no is a very positive thing.

Because time, money, and energy are precious commodities, you owe it to yourself to spend them wisely. The more of these resources you channel into projects that have meaning for you, the more fulfilled and inspired you'll feel. When you stop investing the better part of yourself doing things you don't want to do with people you don't want to see, you will be able to move closer to whatever it is that speaks to your own core beliefs, priorities, and passions. Developing the art of saying no frees up room for the "yeses" in your life.

When saying no becomes a comfortable habit—something you feel justified doing, not something you fear—you'll have acquired a skill that will lead to lifelong satisfaction and a more permanent sense of joy. While you can cope with a busy schedule by making lists and becoming more organized, learning how to manage your time better doesn't really address the whole problem. Saying no is a way to pare down the list and create a much-needed sense of spaciousness and calm.

All of us need a little time to pursue happiness, however we define the word. That's not a luxury; it's a necessity. And learning to say no can help you reclaim it.

## Now, Go No!

The authors would like to assure you that each of the suggestions in this book was designed to be as reasonable, polite, and respectful as possible. We ran them through our guilt filter and they came out clean, so don't be afraid to use them. With very few exceptions, their aim is not to "teach someone a lesson" or take people to task for disturbing you but to help you get through an uncomfortable situation gracefully.

Of course, not every response will be appropriate for every encounter. "I'd sooner die" might not be the best way to turn down a date. But then again . . . we don't know who's asking. We trust you'll use your best judgment.

# 1 Saying No: The Basics

...............................................................................................

*I really don't want to spend Saturday night baby-sitting
my neighbor's three kids. But when she asked me, I didn't
know what to say. So I just said yes. I wish I'd had time
to think of an excuse.*

*Damn! I should have known Mike would hit me up for
a loan. Why did I ever tell him about getting that bonus
check?*

*In my family, there's some kind of event going on nearly
every weekend. Sometimes I just want to stay home and
do nothing. But that doesn't seem like a good enough reason. Unless I have something else on the calendar, I feel
obligated to say yes.*

In this chapter we'll show you a few basic techniques that can
help you say no more easily and avoid regrets like these.

To build up your courage for those really difficult "no's,"
start small. Practice saying no in nonthreatening encounters
where there isn't much at stake. Tell your best friend you don't
want to go to her choice of restaurant, and suggest another.
Tell your husband you don't want to go to the hardware store
with him. Tell your son he can't have more dessert. The object
is to hear yourself saying no successfully. Little by little, stretch
yourself by saying no in more challenging circumstances.

As you begin to develop the healthy habit of saying no,

you'll find the process gets easier all the time. Most likely, you will settle on a few different phrases that work for you and that can be applied to the situations you face most often. The more you use them, the more comfortable you'll become with them. Over time, you will utter them with confidence and ease.

## Basic Principles

There are a couple of basic principles woven through this book that we'd like to emphasize here.

First, saying no without guilt is much easier for all concerned when it's done in the context of *generosity*. This means being helpful and available to family, friends, co-workers, and neighbors whenever you possibly can—in other words, when it won't cause significant stress or inconvenience and when you can say yes without resentment. Just as important, give yourself a little credit for being a generous person. Recognizing the many things you do for others with a willing spirit, you'll feel more confident and less guilty at times when you really do want to say no to them.

The second basic principle of saying no: *Less is more.* The most powerful and effective "no's" are the least complicated, but most of us have a great deal of difficulty saying no politely and leaving it at that. Whether we're telling the boss we can't work late or telling a neighbor we can't walk his dog, we feel obliged to justify our "no" with a detailed explanation—often a fictitious one. Yet elaborating is seldom necessary, and it leaves you on shaky ground. The more specific information you supply, the more likely the other person will be to: a) try to figure out a way to "solve the problem" so that you can actually do the thing he wants you to do (which, of course, you *don't* want to do), b) decide that your reason for saying no isn't good enough and be miffed about it, or c) catch you in a lie (if you're lying).

On the other hand, when you make a statement like "I'm

sorry, I won't be able to" or "I'm afraid I'm busy that day," you sound clear and decisive. If the other person insists on knowing why, the burden of prying will be on him. When that happens, don't fall into the trap of trying to come up with new, more creative excuses to satisfy someone who can't take no for an answer. Instead, repeat yourself as often as necessary. You can emphasize different words, change the language around a bit, or offer some other vague comment. "I'm busy that day" can also be expressed as "I've got plans," "I have a previous engagement," "I've got an appointment I can't break," or "I've had something on my calendar for weeks." Hold your ground in the face of a rude, nosy, or aggressive person. No one has the right to force you to violate your own privacy.

This doesn't mean it's a mistake to tell people the reason you're saying no. Especially when the relationship is a close one, it doesn't feel natural to be too cryptic. But remember that by keeping explanations to a minimum and repeating yourself as often as necessary, you'll be in a stronger position.

## Basic Techniques

Now let's look at the basic techniques every good naysayer should have in her repertoire. Throughout the following chapters, you'll find numerous ideas for using these basics to say no like a pro:

### 1. Buying Time

If you do nothing else suggested in this book, acquire the habit of buying time before responding to requests. It takes the pressure off when you can't figure out how to say no diplomatically or simply need more time to decide. A few stock "time-buying" responses will cover you in just about every situation. For example:

- *I need to check my calendar; I'll get back to you.*

- *Let me check with my husband/wife/partner to see if we're free that day.*
- *I've got to think about that; I'll let you know.*
- *I've got to take a look at my cash flow.*
- *I need to find out if I have to work first.*

## 2. "The Policy"

We love to say no with the phrase "I have a policy." For example, suppose a friend asks for a loan you don't want to extend. Utter the phrase *Sorry, I have a policy about not lending money,* and your refusal immediately sounds less personal.

In all kinds of situations, invoking a policy adds weight and seriousness when you need to say no. It implies that you've given the matter considerable thought on a previous occasion and learned from experience that what the person is requesting is unwise. It can also convey that you've got a prior commitment you can't break. When you turn down an invitation by saying, "Sorry, I can't come—it's our policy to have dinner together as a family every Friday night," it lets the other person know that your family ritual is carved in stone.

Of course, when searching for your response, it helps to *have* a policy. Which brings us to an important point: Saying no comfortably and without guilt requires you to really think about what you stand for. *Why* are you saying no? As you learn to eliminate unwanted obligations from your life, what are you making room *for*? When you can identify and embrace your priorities and focus on what you want *more* of—for example, time with the family, money for an important project or cause—you feel more justified saying no in order to pursue those goals.

## 3. Prevention

Quite simply, this means "Don't be in the wrong place at the wrong time." In the martial arts, it is a cornerstone of self-defense. If you don't want to be struck, you shouldn't plant your body in the path of the oncoming fist. If you don't want to be hit by a train, stay off the railroad tracks. This isn't as glib or simplistic as it sounds. Think about it, and you'll realize you have the power to avoid a good many uncomfortable situations that cry out for an emphatic "no!" Some examples:

- A male friend is pressuring you for a sexual relationship, and you're not interested. *Preventive tactic:* Meet him in a public place, with other people—not alone at his apartment.
- In the supermarket with your six-year-old, the cereal aisle is a battleground: If you don't buy her the Super Sugar Puffs she sees advertised on TV, she throws a tantrum. *Preventive tactic:* Take advantage of every opportunity to stock up on the brands you prefer, so that when you're with your child, you can avoid the cereal aisle entirely.
- You desperately need some time to decompress from your stressful job, so you decide to take a day off to relax at home. And you *really* want that day to yourself—no lunch dates with friends, no shopping with Mom, no calls from co-workers. *Preventive tactics:* Don't tell Mom that you're taking time off if you don't want to spend that time with her. Withholding information is a classic preventive tactic! At home, let your answering machine do its job and keep the world at bay for a day.

As you see, it's a simple idea. Prevention doesn't offer complete control over every situation, but it *can* make a difference.

## 4. "I Have Plans": A New Definition

Broadening your definition of what it means to "have plans" is a liberating experience. Many people feel awkward about refusing an invitation when they don't have another prior engagement on the calendar. But if you really need a night alone at home to take a bubble bath and read a good book, that's a plan. If you really want to spend Saturday playing

Frisbee with your dog or watching videos with your kids, that's a plan. Free, unstructured time is important for relieving stress or bonding with loved ones. Don't be afraid to claim yours.

Give yourself permission to make plans with yourself. If you need to, pencil them into your calendar. Treat them like important dates—because they are.

## 5. Face-Saving Excuses

This book is designed to help you say no—not lie your way out of doing things you don't want to do. However (here comes the big qualifier), it would be foolish to think that telling the whole truth all the time is a wise way to go. Brutal honesty may be just the thing if you're doing an intervention and trying to convince someone to check into rehab. But if you're turning down a date with a guy you find really unattractive, it's a little *too* powerful. Telling him you're involved with someone else, even if it's not quite true, isn't such a terrible sin—it's an act of mercy. That's why a Face-Saving Excuse, deftly delivered, is an important tool of last resort. Use Face-Saving Excuses when they're appropriate for the situation—in other words, when they will spare someone from hurt or embarrassment, make your life easier, and when you won't get caught!

## Preparing to Say No

If the suggestions in this book are going to be of any help whatsoever, you have to be able to say them. But what if you're too plagued by guilt or fear to open your mouth?

Saying no without guilt is a matter of mind over meekness. A little mental preparation will make the task less intimidating. Here is some advice that will get you ready to say no with greater confidence.

## 1. Consider the Many "No's" You've Weathered

We've all been on the receiving end. Surely you've had invitations turned down, been denied favors or privileges, experienced some romantic disappointments. In the end, was it really so terrible? Did you end up hating the person who said no to you? No, you probably survived, maybe even thrived. Your own ability to weather life's ongoing "no's" is proof that people can withstand all kinds of rejection and move on. So don't assume you're going to inflict serious harm by saying no to somebody.

## 2. Learn to Take No for an Answer

This one is for everybody who read the previous item and said, "Yes, it *was* terrible! I *do* hate the person who said no to me!" If you've had some bad experiences, your personal baggage may be causing you to overestimate how badly someone else will react when *you* say no. But try not to let residual hurt from unrelated incidents prevent you from saying no when you need to. The cruel, insensitive characters from your past who still haunt you—teachers, ex-boyfriends, bosses, and (shock!) even parents—are not you. And saying no today, to other people in your life, will not make *you* a cruel, insensitive character, because you are going to say it compassionately, and for all the right reasons. Right?

We hope so. Gain a little perspective by becoming aware of how often people around you say no to each other from day to day. When you really pay attention, you'll find that it happens all the time, and in most cases it's no big deal. Keep that in mind when it's your turn to say no in similar situations, and when someone's saying it to you.

Learn to take "no's" in stride and accept them graciously as a normal part of life. You'll become less agitated about saying no to others, and you'll also be modeling the kind of behavior you hope everyone will adopt.

## 3. Learn from Others

Some people are so good at saying no that you hardly notice they're saying it. Their words sound natural and honest. They adopt a friendly, sympathetic tone of voice. They make eye contact. All these factors help make their "no's" sound like perfectly reasonable, acceptable responses. Others have a way of making everything sound like a harsh rebuke. Observe how different people say no and learn from them. Borrow phrases and mannerisms from the people who say it most pleasantly. Be aware that the *way* you speak often has a more lasting impact than the actual words you use.

## 4. Vocalize!

Are you afraid of the sound of your own voice? It may seem ridiculous—of course, you talk all the time—but in intimidating situations many people find it especially hard to speak up for themselves. They have a built-in fear of making too much noise, so little "meep-meep" sounds come out instead (translation: "Yes, okay, whatever you say"). That's why the authors recommend regular, vigorous exercise for the vocal cords! Get in your car, pop in a tape of your favorite diva (you can't do better than Aretha singing "Respect"), crank up the volume, and sing along at the top of your lungs. Go to your kid's soccer game and scream like a banshee. Or take a karate class and work on those "kiai" yells until they're at black-belt volume. Make a racket!

Then get down to business. Pick out some "no" responses from this book and practice saying them aloud. Choose a few that you'd like to be able to say to someone you know. Try out different phrasings; change the words around until they start flowing naturally and you can say them confidently. Practice with a tape recorder until the sound of your voice no longer makes you cringe (everybody feels that way). Once you get comfortable hearing yourself speak, it won't be so hard to make yourself heard by others.

### 5. Fake It Till You Make It

You might find the "no" responses in this book very difficult to say at first. If so, try the old reliable "fake it till you make it" trick. Visualize yourself saying no strongly and confidently. Then go ahead and behave as if you really *are* strong and confident. Others will respond to you that way and treat you accordingly. Before you know it, you *will* feel stronger and more confident, and you won't have to pretend anymore.

Popular career advice holds that you should dress for the job you *want*, not the job you *have*. In the same way, you can choose to live the life you *want* to live, rather than settling for the one you *have* and dreaming of a better one. So even if your heart isn't quite in it yet, get out there and say your lines. Change your behavior first, and the self-assurance will come later. Trust us, it works.

## Preparing to Say Yes: The Inspiration File

One of the tragedies of a too-busy life is that it can distract you from remembering what it is in this world that truly excites you. In order to get closer to your favorite sources of joy, you need to remind yourself what they are in the first place.

One technique for doing this on a regular basis is something we call the Inspiration File. It simply means collecting little reminders in a folder, scrapbook, or a drawer of your desk of what you'd love to do if only you had more time and energy. Write notes to yourself, jot down ideas, make lists, save pictures, or clip articles about anything that makes you sigh and say, "I wish . . ."

Let's say you've always wanted to travel to Japan. One day    17 you find a lovely photo of Mount Fuji in a travel magazine. That's a perfect item to cut out and place in your Inspiration File. If you fantasize about playing the violin like Isaac Stern, save a course listing from a music school—even if you don't have time to sign up just yet. Open your Inspiration File often, and add items to it whenever you can. Every time you look through what you've saved, imagine yourself moving closer and closer to what draws you. Allow your dream to gestate and take hold. When you keep your eyes on the prize and your dream in focus, you may find that it becomes a little bit more attainable every day.

Here's a true story that illustrates how keeping a little inspiration nearby can lead to a big lifestyle change.

Not too many years ago, Patti was an editor in Manhattan, living in a studio apartment and riding the subway every day to her job in a midtown office building. As she sat at her desk, she would flip through her Sierra Club calendar, lingering over the dramatic shots of majestic mountains and shimmering rivers. "*That's* where I want to be," she'd say, sighing wistfully.

Eventually it occurred to her that she could do more than daydream—she could actually *join* the Sierra Club and explore the glories of nature for herself. Which she did. Before long she was leaving the city nearly every weekend to trek over the mountains and trails of the Northeast. Ultimately Patti's passion for the outdoors became so important in her life that it helped her make a major decision: She left her job, moved to Northern California, and eventually started her own business from home. Now, instead of a picture, she can look up from her desk and see a *real* mountain (okay, a large hill), and she can hike it whenever she likes.

It all started with a calendar—and a little inspiration.

Consider the countless ways that saying no can enhance *your* life and bring you closer to your dreams. Now that you've learned the basics, it's time to get specific. In the following chapters, you will learn the art of saying no to family and kids, friends and neighbors, co-workers, panhandlers, phone solicitors, and others who may want more than you can comfortably give.

# 2 Saying No to Requests for Money

........................................................

*I lent my daughter seventy-five hundred dollars to help
with her down payment on a house. That was five years
ago, and she hasn't paid back a penny yet.*

*This guy in my office never has enough cash when we go
out for a drink after work. He earns as much as I do, so
why am I always covering for him?*

HUNGRY, HOMELESS, ANYTHING APPRECIATED. GOD BLESS.
                                    —Seen on a cardboard sign

Do you want to give away some money? Just look around, and
you'll find plenty of folks eager to take it off your hands.
There's the downtrodden guy on the street who could use a
handout. There's the voice on the phone telling you why her
organization desperately needs your support. Perhaps you'd
like to bail out a relative who's about to go under from debt.
For aspiring philanthropists, the choices are many and their
range mind-boggling.

But even philanthropists need to say no occasionally to
people requesting money. For those times when you're less inclined to reach for your wallet, it pays to think about what
your response will be and develop your "no" skills. Since bad
feelings can arise so easily when money is involved, responding in a compassionate, nonjudgmental way can help minimize
the discomfort factor—for *both* of you.

# Friends Indeed: Fielding Requests for a Loan

In a perfect world, nobody would need to ask a friend or relative for a loan. In an almost-perfect world, every person who asked for a loan would be responsible and trustworthy, repaying the debt in full and on time, with interest. Then there's the not-so-perfect world. If that's where you live, you need to know how to say no.

## The Price of Friendship?

If you're wary about lending money to someone, there's a good chance your trepidation isn't really about money. More likely it's about the *baggage* that goes with it.

When Kate decided to extend a loan to a friend in crisis, she realized she would probably never see that money again. For years her friend Amy, a struggling actress, had been unable to find and keep steady work. She managed to eke out a living through infrequent, low-paying acting jobs, while being heavily subsidized by a family member and a series of boyfriends. That support eventually dried up, and Amy's situation became worse; the bills piled up, her phone and electricity were turned off, and she risked losing her home altogether.

While Kate believed that Amy had only herself to blame for her predicament, she felt compelled to help her friend through the immediate crisis with a loan of several thousand dollars—knowing full well that Amy, who already had many debts, wasn't likely to pay it back.

She was right, of course.

In the months that followed, Kate saw her friend bounce back from the crisis and resume her fun-loving ways. She began dating a successful man, ate in good restaurants, took a vacation, and spent most of her days sleeping late, shopping, and seeing friends. This infuriated Kate. She knew that if the situation were reversed, she would do anything—take any job—until she repaid her debt. Kate found herself in an unhappy position: She could keep hounding her friend for the money or write it off altogether. She suspected that Amy considered repayment a low priority, because Kate had a well-paying job. Amy, on the other hand, *always* needed money.

Though Kate had always known that Amy was irresponsible, in an optimistic little corner of her heart she'd hoped that her friend would come through for her. Until money changed hands, Amy's careless habits were her own business, almost an amusing character trait. But when Kate, too, became a creditor, she couldn't help but judge her friend's self-indulgent lifestyle much more harshly than before. Now she had a personal interest at stake. Her anger over Amy's behavior caused their relationship to turn a corner, because an essential ingredient of friendship had been destroyed: trust. While she never really missed the funds from her bank account, Kate felt betrayed. She was offended that Amy had taken advantage of her and failed to live up to her end of the bargain.

It may or may not be true that money changes everything . . . but it sure can mess up a relationship. As this story illustrates, a personal loan is often more than a mere financial transaction. If money were the only issue, the decision would be simple: Either you have enough to lend or you don't. End of story.

Even if you've got plenty of money, however, you may still hesitate. How do you feel about the person borrowing it? Is he likely to pay it back or at least try to? What does he need the money for? In a sense, being asked for a loan invites you to sit in judgment over the person requesting it, to size up his character, his need, and decide whether he's worthy. If for some reason you disapprove of his behavior—if you believe he wound up in a jam due to laziness or carelessness—you are *not* going to be a cheerful giver.

People sometimes feel guilty about saying no to a loan request when they do have ample money to lend, especially if the other person *knows* they've got it. Granted, it's an awkward situation to be put in, and you'll resent the fact you were even asked. But if you're trapped into lending money against your will, you'll resent it even more.

## Saying No to Requests for Sizable Loans

Say no to requests for money in simple language, without offering a reason for your decision. Supplying limited information puts the onus on the other person to pursue the issue further. *No. I wish I could, but I can't. It's just not possible. Sorry.* With luck, he'll drop it right there. If you need to say more, try one of the following.

### Face-Saving Excuses: "I Can't Afford It"
Saying no because you're short of funds removes the personal element from your decision; for the loan-seeker, it's a less embarrassing way to be turned down. Even if it stretches the truth a bit, in certain cases you might imply that you're saying no for financial reasons. Again, keep it simple.

- *Sorry; this just isn't a good time for me to be lending money.*
- *My finances are such that I wouldn't be comfortable lending money right now.*
- *Sorry, I can't. Because I'm self-employed, my income fluctuates and I need to make sure I have enough to get through my slow times.*

### The Policy: "Friends and Loans Don't Mix"
- *Sorry, I have a strict policy about not lending money to friends. I just think it's a bad idea.*
- *I don't believe in lending money to friends unless it's a dire emergency. Since this isn't one, I have to say no.*
- *Your friendship is really important to me, which is why I'm not comfortable lending you money. I think it would change the nature of our relationship to have you in debt to me. I'd rather not open that can of worms.*

### Gifts: "Don't Pay Me Back"

At times you might prefer to give all or part of the requested amount as a gift rather than as a loan. The advantage of a gift is that it relieves both of you from the pressure of worrying about repayment. But don't do this unless you can offer it freely and without resentment.

- *No, I don't lend money but I'll give you a gift. I can give you _____. I hope that helps.*
- *I can give you _____. But instead of paying me back, I'd rather you give the money directly to charity.*

### Between Generations: "Hands Off My Nest Egg"

Years ago one of the authors asked her father to help with the down payment on a house. She was promptly told, "Forget it. You shouldn't be buying a house you can't afford." After a brief hissy fit, she decided that Dad had a point. He also had the right to preserve his savings for his own future. And so do you. When your grown children ask for loans you don't feel comfortable extending, tell them:

- *I've been saving that money for my retirement. There are plenty of things I want to use it for. I'm sorry, but you'll have to find another way to make that down payment.*
- *Sorry, but no. I don't believe people should live beyond their means. If you can't convince a bank to lend you the money, I don't want to lend it either.*
- *As much as I love you and want you to be happy, I'm not going to give you the loan. You're old enough to be paying your own way.*

Remember that when someone catches you off guard with a loan request, you can always buy time to think about your answer by saying, *I've got to check my finances* or simply, *Let me think about it and get back to you.*

If you do choose to lend money, be smart and put it in writing. Should the borrower balk at this or seem offended that you even brought it up, consider that a big red flag. A letter of agreement spelling out the terms of your loan is the best protection for your relationship, because it will help you avoid any misunderstandings down the line. (It also confirms that the loan is a "real" transaction, in case anyone were inclined to forget.) It doesn't have to be fancy or complicated, and you don't need a lawyer—just a simple statement indicating the amount of the loan, the interest you're charging (if any), and a schedule for repayment. Make two copies, signed by both of you, one for each of you to keep.

## Saying No to a Mooch

The mooch is not a big financial drain—instead, he's like a slow, steady drip. We all know mooches. They're the people who hit you up for a dollar here, a dollar there, until it becomes a way of life. They don't have any cash when the coffee wagon comes around at the office. When you're out together, they're caught short and can't *quite* pay their share. They never have the right change for the bus and need to bum it from you. They never pay you back, but you're too embarrassed to protest. Each little incident, taken by itself, seems *so* trivial. But together, like that steady drip, drip, drip in your sink, they can sure drive you crazy. Which is why the mooch must be stopped. Suggestions follow.

### Face-Saving Excuses: "I Can't Afford It"
- *Not today; I'm short on cash.* (Say it often enough and you'll eventually make your point.)
- *Actually, I was just about to ask you for the five dollars I lent you last week.*

### The Policy: "Friends and Loans Don't Mix"
- *I've made a new policy. I'm not lending money to anybody anymore. My cash disappears too fast as it is.*
- *Sorry, no more loans. Because I'm beginning to resent this, and I don't want to resent you.*

### Teasing: "The Bank Is Closed, Mooch"

- *You've already reached your credit limit with me. I'm going to have to send a collection agency after you.*
- *Sing* "I Can't Give You Anything but Love."
- YOU: *I'll lend you three dollars if you come wash my bathtub.*
  MOOCH: *What do you mean?*
  YOU: *You're becoming a sponge!*

Preventive tactics can also help keep a mooch at bay. For example, before dining out together, ask him, *Do you need to stop at the cash machine first?* or *Did you remember your credit card?* To convey that you don't have enough cash to lend, when you sit down at the restaurant, say something like *I'd better make sure I have enough money with me before I order the Deluxe Platter.*

## Saying No to "The Opportunity of a Lifetime"

If you haven't yet been approached by someone wanting you to get involved in a multilevel marketing (MLM) operation, it's probably only a matter of time.

With MLM, also known as network marketing, distributors are recruited to sell a particular line of products (such as cleaning supplies or vitamins) to friends, family, neighbors, co-workers, and anyone else who will listen. However, if you've ever heard an MLM sales pitch, you know that the biggest moneymaking potential comes not from product sales but from bringing other people into the company. That's because the original distributor then gets to collect a cut from the sales of everyone he's sponsored, and everyone they've sponsored, and so on down the line.

Ultimately, whether or not to get involved with an MLM is a personal decision. Our view is that, among other things, we're not wild about any business that encourages people to exploit their personal relationships for money. Salespeople have the right to ask once, and everyone has the right (and, we hope, the skills) to say no in response.

Multilevel marketers often recruit new distributors through meetings held in their homes, hotels, or other locations. If you go, you'll probably be subjected to a slick presentation and lots of motivational pep talk designed to suck you in. The best resistance is to avoid going to the meeting in the first place. When invited to one, say:

- *No thanks. I'm not interested.*
- *Frankly, I just don't want to get involved, and attending the meeting will not change my mind. Thanks anyway.*

### When the Pitch Begins

- *You seem very excited, and I wish you lots of luck with it. But it's not for me. I wouldn't enjoy it, and I wouldn't be good at it. Thanks anyway.*
- *I don't like selling. If I did, I would have gone into sales as my profession and probably made a lot more money! I simply have no interest in either selling the products or enlisting other people to sell them.*
- *They seem like good products. I'll buy some _____ from you because it's something I use regularly. But beyond that, I don't want to get involved.*
- *I already turned down this opportunity before when someone else asked me, and I haven't changed my mind.*
- *You're very persistent. I see why you're such a successful salesperson. But I've said no. Please don't ask me again.*

## Saying No to People and Organizations in Need

While this book is about saying no, it is not our goal to discourage generosity toward people in need, charities, or other worthy causes. In fact, we want to nurture every altruistic impulse that presents itself. The key to saying no without guilt to these requests for money is to know in your heart that you're a generous person. And the way to feel like a generous person is to give like one. So if you're not already supporting at least one cause or organization you truly believe in, why not start now?

Depending on your available resources, you can contribute money, time, or both. Do it in an organized, conscious way, and make a commitment you'll be able to live with. It's not difficult to locate worthwhile programs or organizations in need of whatever you can offer. You can find them through your church, synagogue, or local religious institutions. If you read in a magazine or newspaper about a group that's working for a cause you'd like to support, call them up. Or call the local volunteer center for a referral.

Another way to focus your charitable giving is to collect all the direct-mail appeals you receive for a few months. Then review them carefully, and consider which resonate most with you. Maybe your mother died of cancer, and you want to remember her with an annual donation to cancer research. Perhaps you feel a need to touch the lives of people living on the streets of your community, in which case you can volunteer at a soup kitchen or contribute to the social services that work with the homeless, mentally ill, or addicted. Or maybe you want to support an educational program for disadvantaged kids, to give them more of a fair shake in society. Devote your whole contribution to one important cause, or split it among many. It's up to you. But whatever you do, you'll have the satisfaction of knowing you're making a difference, and that's very gratifying. (Before you donate any money, however, it's a good idea to do a background check on the organizations you're considering. See the sidebar on page 29 for more information.)

If you have a focused passion—a cause that lights up your eyes and delights you with a vision for the future—you will be making a contribution to that vision every time you support that cause. The more committed you are to supporting the causes close to your heart, the easier it will be to say no to other people's causes.

# Are Those Charities *Really* Appealing?

. . . . . . . . . . . . . . . . . . . . . . . . . . . . . . . . . . . . . . . . . . . . . . . . . . . . . . .

Before you mail that check, make sure the charity you're considering is a reputable one and that you haven't been misled about its true purpose. It should operate like a well-run business and deliver a sizable percentage of your contribution directly to the cause you're supporting (rather than to administrative costs).

Your local Better Business Bureau can provide information about nonprofit organizations in your area. To learn more about national charities, consult one or more of the following information sources:

**Philanthropic Advisory Service (PAS) of the Council of Better Business Bureaus, Inc.**
www.bbb.org/about/pas
Designed to educate donors so they can make informed decisions, PAS supplies information on hundreds of nonprofit organizations and their programs, governance, fund-raising practices, and finances. Looks at performance based on its Standards for Charitable Solicitations.

**National Charities Information Bureau (NCIB)**
19 Union Square West
New York, NY 10003
(212) 929-6300
www.give.org
Like PAS, the NCIB evaluates charities based on a defined set of standards, in this case the NCIB Standards in Philanthropy. It maintains an on-line guide to four hundred charities and offers a free "Wise Giving Guide." You can also order reports—the first one is free; additional reports cost $3.50.

**GuideStar**
www.guidestar.org
This free on-line service maintains a database of information on more than six hundred thousand charities and nonprofits. You can research an organization's programs and finances and get news on philanthropy and resources for donors and volunteers.

## Saying No to Charitable Solicitations

Like us, you probably receive a great number of solicitations each year to contribute to a variety of worthwhile causes. If you read the direct-mail appeals or listen to the phone callers, it can be hard to turn away and say no. But while you can't say yes to every request for money, you can make a commitment to more mindful giving, based on your own personal beliefs and priorities.

Once you've established the habit of generosity, you will still have to decline some requests for money from people with genuine needs. Here are some "no" responses we have found useful:

- *I'm sorry, all my charitable contributions have been allocated for the year.*
- *Sorry, I can't. I give all my money to* _____. (Fill in the blank with your organization or cause of choice, e.g., "I give all my money to cancer research.")
- *My family and I plan our charitable donations once a year in December. If you'd like to send some literature, we'll consider it.*
- *Sorry. I have a policy not to respond to solicitations over the phone.* (If you like, tell them to contact you by mail and that you will review their information at a later date.)

## Cute Little Fund-raisers

For some people, like our friend Susan, the most dreaded encounter with donation-seekers takes place in front of the supermarket. That's where, more often than not, she's accosted by a couple of adorable ten-year-old fund-raisers who'd like her to support their school, soccer team, or youth program.

"I can't stand it!" says Susan. "It seems like they're *always* there, every time I go shopping. Of course they're collecting for worthwhile reasons, and that's admirable. But I just hate feeling like I *have* to give them money all the time. When I walk on by, I feel terrible—like I'm the worst person in the world."

The situation makes her uncomfortable enough that she's gone so far as to rearrange her errands, going elsewhere first and coming back later to shop after the kids have gone. At other times she's felt compelled to explain to them that she wasn't carrying any cash, only credit cards.

So young, so innocent—with all that power. It's frightening. Who wouldn't want to support these kids in their efforts? Who can deny their earnest requests?

*You* can.

Think of it this way: When you were young, didn't your mother teach you that you can't always get what you want? (If she didn't, the Rolling Stones must have.) These kids are absorbing that lesson, too. In the course of the day, plenty of people will pass their table without stopping and reaching for change. You might be one of them, and if you are, well, so be it. No fund-raiser, however young and naive, however cute and sweet, can expect contributions from 100 percent of the pool. That's reality, and the nature of fund-raising. So next time they make their appeal, if you're not inclined to give, simply look them in the eye, give them a warm, encouraging smile, and say, *Sorry, I can't today—but good luck!*

## Brother, Can You Spare a Dime?

How often are you approached on the street by someone asking for a handout? A few times a year? Several times a day? Do you reach into your pocket and pull out some change? Or do you walk on without looking back?

As we all know only too well, there are a lot of people in need living in our communities—and not just in the big cities. They're also in suburbia, small towns, and rural areas. Just as

## "Found Money" for a Good Cause

A woman we know discovered an easy way to set aside a little extra for charity. She collects all the "found money" that comes into her life, saving it in a jar until there's enough to make up a donation to a cause she cares about.

Think of "found money" as any funds that come your way that you weren't expecting, or at least weren't counting on. Aside from cash you literally "find"—e.g., in an old coat pocket or on the street—here are some other places to look for "found money":

- Gifts (Is Aunt Gloria still sending you ten dollars for your birthday?)
- Winnings from an office pool, card game, bingo, or lottery
- All or part of a tax refund
- The price of a magazine subscription you've decided not to renew
- The money you save when you buy something on sale
- Consignment-store money: If you donate clothing or furniture to a consignment shop, you split the profit with the store when your item sells.

Try it—it's painless!

there is no one reason a person might end up begging on the street, there is no one "right" course of action when confronted by a stranger asking for money. So what do you do?

If our informal survey is any indication, responses toward begging vary widely. Some people adopt a policy never to aid anyone panhandling on the street, believing that handouts just perpetuate the problem. We've also met people who like to carry around a roll of quarters from which they can hand out change all week. Others offer to buy food in lieu of giving money. Often people react "in the moment"; they try to size up each individual very quickly, relying on transitory, rather vague impressions to formulate a snap decision. Is he truly in need, or is he hustling me? Will she use the money for drugs? Is he faking illness or disability to arouse my sympathy?

Even those of us who are predisposed to help aren't consistent. Sometimes we're in a hurry, we don't want to dig for change, or we're simply not up to facing someone in such desperate straits. It disturbs us; we want to get away fast and forget about it. But often we're left with a nagging feeling. Did we just pass up a world-class con man or the saddest, neediest, most vulnerable person in the world? When we're with our children, we worry about the example we're setting. For one reason or another, we come away feeling guilty—maybe not every time, but often enough to bother us.

If you're completely comfortable with the way you handle these encounters, you're a rare individual—and you probably don't need to read this section. But most of us fall somewhere along the continuum between Scrooge and Mother Teresa, and there in the middle things look a little fuzzy. We believe in helping others; we want to be compassionate. But we hate and resent the intrusion and the confrontational aspect of being approached by a stranger.

There's nothing wrong with saying no to a panhandler, but you'll both feel better if you say it kindly. A few simple words are all you need.

- *Sorry.*
- *Not today.*
- Shrug/show empty palms and say any of following: *Good luck to you. Be well. God bless.*

If you want to do more than just refuse, it might require doing a little homework about the resources available in your community.

- *Here's a food voucher.* (These coupons are sold in many communities; they can be given to indigent people and redeemed for groceries at local markets.)

- *Do you know about the food pantry? They offer free groceries/hot meals every day.* (Provide address.)

When you pass a person begging on the street, however you choose to respond, it's important to keep in mind that the person you're facing is a human being. Too often beggars are spat upon, cursed, mugged, or ignored. Just a smile or nod can improve someone's day.

In the context of a life grounded in generosity and compassion, saying no to certain requests for money needn't afflict you with self-reproach. When you're enthusiastically supporting one or more causes that reflect *your* convictions and advance *your* dreams for this world, you'll have plenty to feel good—not guilty—about.

# 3 Saying No at Work

A. *I love my work. If I hit the lottery tomorrow, I'd keep working, because if I stopped, I'd feel a void in my life.*

B. *Depends on what day you ask me, but work is usually not too bad.*

C. *I work for money, period. (And I buy plenty of lottery tickets.)*

Whatever kind of work you do, your attitude toward your job can probably be summed up with one of the statements above. If you chose A, congratulations on being one of the fortunate few. But if you're like most people we know, your feelings about your job fall somewhere between "It's basically okay" (B) and "Get me outta here" (C).

There's absolutely nothing wrong with having a "good enough" job. But there *is* something wrong if you habitually allow conditions (or people) in the workplace to leave you angry or bitter at the end of the day. Or if out of passivity or fear you let the job consume your life, keeping you from the people and things you love and preventing you from pursuing your dreams. If you're unhappy at work, it's hard to feel good about anything else. That's why when it comes to the workplace, mastering the fine art of saying no is absolutely essential.

Knowing how to say no on the job—and, when necessary, no *to* the job—can make a world of difference in your quality of life. It helps keep the day-to-day stresses under control. But more important, setting reasonable limits on your hours and workload gives you more opportunities to carve out a full, satisfying life *beyond* work. Strengthening your resolve to say no can bring you closer to what you want to say yes to. Reflecting that balance, this chapter provides many specifics for saying no on the job, while also keeping the larger picture in sight.

In the following pages you'll find suggested "no" responses for a wide variety of situations that may upset your on-the-job equilibrium: long hours, excessive workload, unreasonable requests, as well as rudeness, harassment, and safety issues. Later we'll discuss strategies for keeping your dreams alive and nourishing your spirit no matter what you do for a living. We'll also look at how more and more people are rethinking their entire approach to moneymaking in favor of a simpler life and entrepreneurial ventures that allow them more independence and self-determination.

## Today's Employee: Stretched and Squeezed

Is there any such thing as a nine-to-five job anymore? In most offices, it seems to have gone the way of the manual typewriter and carbon paper. The idea of heading out the door at 5 P.M.—guilt-free and unburdened by "homework"—seems like a fantasy from an earlier, simpler time. Somehow, when we weren't looking, the eight-hour workday quietly stretched and stretched and stretched—stretching us along with it. The nine-to-five workweek *does* still exist . . . but now it's considered a part-time job! In a 1998 article, the *New York Times* cited a study indicating that about one-third of the salaried *part-time* employees surveyed spent at least thirty-five hours on the job.

It's ironic that so many people seem to be working harder at a time when new technology should be making our lives easier. But in many ways computers, fax machines, voice mail, e-mail, and cell phones only increase the pressure. Now you're expected to do a lot more, and to do it faster and without an assistant (though if you're lucky, you may get to share one with six other people).

It's true the advances that have transformed the workplace have also opened the door to a new array of work options, such as flextime, telecommuting, and entrepreneurship, in record numbers. But all these technical capabilities can also make it harder to escape the job. When it's so easy to stay in touch with the office and with clients—when we can zap a document to the other side of the world in an instant—what *can't* we do? This wonderful digital age allows us to drag a laptop computer along on vacation, where we can now focus on writing memos instead of gazing out at the sea. Instead of listening to the rhythm of crashing waves, we can pull out our cell phone and check in for messages. Lucky us!

In the pursuit of greater profits and productivity, even "nice guys"—and nice companies—can make unreasonable demands on employees. It might even happen before you realize it, because management has such a nice, warm, familial way of squeezing you. They'll give you a plaque inscribed with the company's mission statement. They'll call a meeting and talk about your shared goals, emphasizing that each employee is an important member of the team. And being the good team player that you are, you want to achieve those goals. You want to perform like a hero and *win the game!*

Well, that's fine. Work is more fun when your energy level is up and you feel excited about what you're doing. But don't let the motivational speeches sweep you off your feet—or worse, make you feel guilty about saying no when you need to reclaim some time for yourself.

You'll manage the guilt a lot better if you can maintain a healthy perspective about what a corporate job really means in this day and age. As you've probably noticed, there are no guarantees in this post-downsizing era. Despite what they might have told you at the latest pep rally, the company's priority is to look after its bottom line—not to look after you.

So keep that in mind the next time you start to blame yourself for leaving work "early" at 5 P.M. to pick up your kids from the baby-sitter. And think twice before you invest 110 percent of yourself in the job, at the expense of your family, your dreams, or your personal development.

## Employed, Not Enslaved: Saying No on the Job

When the system pushes you too hard, you owe it to yourself to push back. Not because your company is the enemy or because your boss is a cruel person who only wants to exploit you (though that's a possibility). But because your happiness on the job depends on being able to establish fair and sensible boundaries and communicate when enough is enough. First, though, consider whether the person you most need to say no to is yourself.

### Say No to Your Inner Slave Driver

Do you drive yourself harder than any boss ever could?

"I went into my job with the understanding that it was going to require a lot of me," says Melanie, a marketing director in a large corporation. "The department was a mess, and the systems were in really bad shape. At first I was willing to put in the extra hours and worked late every night. Quite a few times I was at the office till one or two in the morning and had to book a hotel room nearby. But I knew I couldn't continue that way. The job was intruding far too much on my personal life and affecting my state of mind. After about nine months I drew the line. I just said, 'You know what? My day is over. I'm going home.'

"The funny thing is, setting those limits didn't create any conflict with my manager. He didn't expect me to keep up those crazy hours. But it created a big conflict within *myself*.

I'm so used to doing whatever it takes to get the job done, that for me to say, 'This is all I can do today,' was tough. It showed me that I'm much harder on myself than anyone else is."

It's not easy being a control freak in an out-of-control workplace. But in today's "stretched and squeezed" environment, overload is often the normal state of affairs. If you're like Melanie, the demands of your position may be so enormous and the workload so heavy that it's simply impossible ever to catch up completely. Once you acknowledge that perfection is an unattainable goal and let go of it, you'll take a big step toward controlling any feelings of inadequacy and guilt you might have when there's a report left unfinished or messages left unanswered at the end of the day.

"Whenever I feel guilty about leaving by six P.M.," says Melanie, "I tell myself, 'Nobody on their deathbed ever wished they had worked longer and harder.' It eases my conscience because I know it's true."

*Your* inner slave driver may be the source of your worst on-the-job pressures. Then again, that honor may go to your boss or to other colleagues. You can say no to them, too . . . but the way you say it makes all the difference.

## Say No with a Positive Spin

Did your mother ever say, "You can catch more flies with honey than with vinegar"? While it's not *always* the best approach, Mom's advice is a very good place to start when it comes to saying no on the job.

As long as there have been jobs, people have complained about them, and you may have good reasons to complain about yours. But if you want to be able to say no when it counts, being perceived as a complainer will work against you. It's important to create a positive context in which you'll be able to say no successfully, so be aware of the image you project. In this arena, your attitude can make or break you. People who are regarded as dedicated and cooperative in the larger sense will have an easier time when they have to say no in a specific situation, so take advantage of opportunities to show you're a team player. You'll face less resistance from managers and co-workers if they know you're willing to go the extra mile at other times.

When you're turning down any kind of request at work, the last thing your colleagues want to hear is a long litany of reasons that you can't help them. Generally the best approach to saying no is to sandwich your response between a sympathetic phrase and a constructive suggestion or compromise. Follow these three steps:

1. Express your overall desire to be helpful.
   - *I wish I could help you* . . .
   - *Normally, I'd be happy to take that on* . . .
   - *Hmmmm, I see your problem; I've been there myself* . . .

2. Explain in *simple terms* the reason you must decline. Stick to the facts, and don't use it as an opportunity to vent about how busy you are.
   - *The boss just gave me a rush project, and I have to put everything else aside till it's done.*
   - *I have got to leave here by five today.*
   - *Because of my other deadlines, I won't be able to get you that information by tomorrow.*

3. Try to be part of the solution. After all, you're all presumably working toward the same goals, aren't you? For example:
   - *Can we talk about it on Wednesday? By then I should be able to give you the time you need.*
   - *Have you thought about hiring a freelancer to help you through this crunch?*
   - *Can you give me an extra day for the Beapo presentation? Then I can focus on this problem and put together something that might help.*

## Saying No to Overtime

In a hectic work environment, where the pressure's always on to go in early, work late, and take work home, it helps to know how to say no to excessive hours on the job. What we're referring to here would be called "overtime" if you got paid for it.

If you suddenly were given one extra hour a day to spend exactly as you pleased, do you know what you would do with it? Would you spend time with the kids, go to the gym, work in the garden, hide out somewhere with a book? Maybe you don't even know; you've never had time to think about it.

Give yourself permission to set realistic limits on the amount of time you work, even when you don't have a personal emergency and even if you don't have kids. Everyone has the right to a private life; what you do with it is your business. Your "other commitments" may be things you do to have fun, stay sane, keep your body in shape, challenge your mind, or nurture your spirit. Your deepest desires need to be honored and deserve to be.

To claim what's rightfully yours—a reasonable workday—we recommend some version of the statement "I have plans." No elaborate explanation is necessary. The danger of supplying too many details is that your manager may feel your "excuse" isn't good enough. It's more effective to say, "I've got an appointment," than to say, "I'm meeting some friends for drinks." If it's important to you, it's important enough. A statement like one of the following should stand on its own:

- *I simply can't put in the time tonight/this weekend because . . .*
  - *I have plans with my family.*
  - *I have another commitment/commitments at home.*
  - *My evening/time/weekend is already spoken for.*
  - *I've got an event that day.*
- *I'll sign up for next week's crisis, but this time I really have to leave.*

41

- *I'm burned out for tonight. I'll be much more productive to-morrow after I've had a good night's sleep.*
- *I can't stay to finish this tonight. I require at least four hours' sleep a night, and if I want to get them, I've got to leave now.*

## Saying No to Overwork

Busy though you may be, it's generally not advisable to say no outright to an assignment that is your responsibility. But you can relieve some of the pressure by encouraging your boss or co-workers to meet you halfway.

### Prevention

At times it's possible to say no to work before it falls on you. There are gracious ways of letting people know when it's not a good time for them to give you an assignment. Ideally, announce this in a group situation, such as a meeting, so it's not directed at any one person. Use this Prevention technique only when it's really justified, and of course, say it in a noncomplaining way: Let them know you're still available for important projects. Say something like:

- *With the sales conference just two weeks away, those of us in the art department will be extra busy rushing to get all your presentations and other materials ready. During this crunch time, we'd really appreciate it if you could hold off on any assignments that aren't absolutely critical.*

### Impossible Deadlines

When given a project that can't possibly be completed by the requested deadline, invite the other person into the planning process and try to work out a solution together.

- *I'm concerned that with all my other deadlines looming, I might not be able to get to this in time. Can we talk about priorities?*

- *I can do it, but only if I put aside this other project. Can we live with that?*

Without ever saying no directly, you may be able to prove on paper that the project in question cannot be completed in the allotted time without some rethinking. Working backward from your deadline, discuss the necessary steps involved (e.g., the need to obtain information or materials from third parties, the number of approvals required, holidays that might delay progress).

- *Just to make sure nothing falls through the cracks, let's work out a timetable for this project.*

Express interest in the project, but negotiate the how and when.

- *This project looks really interesting, and I'd love to work on it. But there's no way I'll be able to do it over the weekend. It's just not possible. Any chance of getting an extension? Otherwise, I could put aside the Squeako project till early next week and have this for you by Tuesday.*

Agree to do it, but let them know they'll have to get in line.

- *I'd be happy to do that. I can have it for you in about three months.*

Agree to do it, but let them know you won't be able to give it as much attention as they (or you) would like.

- *I can look it over quickly and give you my thoughts, but I won't be able to study it in detail or prepare a written report.*

## Saying No to Unreasonable Requests

This is a slippery, subjective area. What seems "unreasonable" to you may seem perfectly fair to the person making the request. (Depending on who that person is, you might not have a lot of choice in the matter.) But there are a number of ways you can respond to an inappropriate request, even if you only succeed in making the other person think twice about imposing on you again.

### When It Falls Outside Your Set of Responsibilities

Refer the person making the request to a more appropriate individual. Avoid saying, "That's not my job." The idea is to help solve the problem, not become another obstacle.

- *Wendy's really the expert on market research. I'm sure she could answer your question more accurately than I could, so I'm going to pass this on to her.*
- *Since I do event planning, I'm not too involved in database management. Let me see if I can find out who you should talk to about that.*
- *I'm not the best person to do the layout for the new brochure. I'm a copywriter, and I don't really have an art background. For something like this, you probably want to bring in a good graphic designer. I can recommend a few if you'd like.*

### When It's Personal, Not Professional

Personal tasks are built in to some job descriptions, so it's important to know whether these responsibilities are expected of you in your position. If they are, it's not appropriate to say no to these requests.

Even when they're not part of your job, performing personal favors such as running errands and fetching coffee for your boss or co-workers may not be a problem for you at all—especially if they're just as likely to return the favor. An atmosphere in which people are happy to help each other out and do so without "pulling rank" is a pleasant place to work. But if someone is pressuring you into personal servitude, because you're either in a subordinate position or just a "nice guy," draw the line.

Often the personal task we're asked to perform is one for which professional services are readily available. Define your own limits by suggesting that the person hire a pro:

- *Sorry, I can't do that. But I'm sure the Quik-E Dry Cleaner will pick up and deliver your suit for you.* (If you want to be helpful, add, *I'll look up the number for you.*)
- *I'm afraid I can't take care of your dog while you're away this weekend. Shall I try to find a pet-sitting service for you?*

For a more direct approach:

- *If I go to your house to feed your cats, it will take me away from my work for at least an hour. That means I won't be able to finish this report for the meeting this afternoon. It's got to be one or the other. How would you rather I spent my time?*
- *If I did this for you, I'd be setting a precedent that I don't want to set.*

OR

- *I'll do it this time, but I don't want to set a precedent.* (Optional: *Let's talk about how we should handle the situation if it comes up again.*)
- *I don't think it's appropriate for you to ask me to do that.*

### When It's a Function You'd Like to Keep at a Distance

- *The job of cleaning up after parties/collecting money for gifts/organizing the softball game seems to have fallen to me. I'm happy to pitch in and do my share, but to be fair, we should all take turns. Someone else can do it this time.*
- *I don't want to become known as the office caterer every time we have a meeting. Let's set up an account with Café Figaro and have them deliver coffee and danish.*

## Saying No to a Dumb Idea

Some projects are a complete waste of time, and some ideas are just plain dumb. Depending on who generates them, your ability to influence the situation may be limited. Diplomacy is key here. Resist the temptation to run down all the reasons the idea stinks. With luck, you'll need just one good reason to make your point! (Smart naysayers choose their battles wisely and go easy on the criticism.) Express your reservations delicately, and compliment some aspect of the idea if at all possible. For example, say you're in charge of planning a party for clients, and your boss has his own "interesting" idea on how to get the word out.

- *That's a really creative idea, Tom—delivering invitations via carrier pigeons, with RSVP cards attached to their legs! One thing concerns me though. Most of our clients work in highrise buildings with windows that can't be opened. How will the birds get in and out?*

Offer to work up some alternate ideas, or suggest another possibility.

- *Since our goal is to promote the company's new birdseed, we could have custom chocolates made up in the shape of a bird, and include one with each invitation. Everyone loves chocolate, so it would get people's attention.*

Other basic techniques will also work here.

- Buy Time: *That's an interesting approach you're suggesting. I'd like to do a little research first and then meet with you again in a day or two to work out the details. Let's make sure we consider all aspects of the program so we'll be prepared for every possible outcome.*
- Prevention: When a dead-in-the-water project looms, lie low. Try not to volunteer to invest your time in something you have little faith in.

### Knowing When Not to Force the Issue

Office politics being what they are, saying no to a bad idea isn't always a good idea.

Rosemary works for a company that plans business conferences. When her manager gave her forty-eight hours to put together a detailed budget for the coming year, she felt that many important questions needed to be answered first.

"It was very frustrating," Rosemary says. "I was being asked to come up with the entire strategy of six conferences within two days, and I had no information to work with. Operating this way means that major business decisions are being made that aren't based on reality." When she voiced her concerns to her boss, he made it clear that he didn't have time to worry about "details." That's because he had to present the budget to *his* manager, who had told *him* to get it done.

Many unreasonable requests emanate from high up the chain of command, which makes the odds of negotiation or compromise pretty slim. Rosemary had little leverage with her boss because he wasn't really the one issuing the assignment. When the person you're dealing with is "stuck in the middle" and must rely on you to make him look good, it adds to the pressure. His stress becomes your stress. In this situation, even though logic was clearly on Rosemary's side, protesting too much would have been a tactical error.

She realized she would have to say yes to this request despite her misgivings, and she did her best with the budget. "There was no point in beating my head against the wall in protest," she says. "He'd see me as negative, not a team player. All I could do was state my concerns and move on."

When you're forced to get involved with a project you consider ill-conceived, the best course is to cover yourself in writing and send copies to all the relevant parties. Try not to sound defensive or accusatory. Adopt a calm, detached, "just the facts" tone.

In this situation, Rosemary wrote something along these lines: "The budget you requested is attached. Please note that because many factors have not yet been determined, I had to make certain assumptions in order to develop my estimates. [These include: . . .] I just want to make sure everyone understands that the more these variables change, the less reliable this budget will be."

## The "Perception Is Everything" Problem

A friend of ours reported that her boss called a meeting and told her staff, "No one in this department is anywhere near a nervous breakdown, so I know you're not working hard enough."

We couldn't have made up a better example of managerial madness if we tried. Did the woman who uttered this statement really believe that her people would be more effective if they worked themselves to the point of mental collapse?

It quickly became clear to her department that this boss's agenda had to do with *perception,* not reality. At the meeting in question, she did not cite one instance of a project's being mishandled or left unfinished. The department's actual competence and productivity were never discussed. What concerned her was the *appearance* of productivity. She believed that if those under her supervision were seen to be working long hours, running around in an agitated state, and maybe throwing an occasional tantrum, it would reflect well on her as a manager. It would signal to *her* boss that she ran a tight ship and got the most out of her people.

Working for someone with values like this could make anyone crazy. But to a large extent, perception *is* reality in the workplace. Like it or not, your success depends not simply on how good a job you do but on how good a job you *appear* to be doing. The way others size you up will be determined by whether you exhibit the traits they consider valuable. (This manager seems to believe that visible stress is the badge of a truly dedicated employee, while composure is the sign of a slacker.)

While most people try to project a certain desired image at work, there is only so much conforming one person can do. Preserving your autonomy is more important than trying to adopt behavior that makes you uncomfortable or conflicts with your values. When up against a perception problem, introduce a little reality of your own by encouraging your boss to focus on what you actually produce, rather than on how you produce it. Using the above example as a model, here are some suggestions.

### The Productivity Argument
- *I do a much better job and am more productive when I can approach things in a calm state. Being stressed out and nervous only makes things more time-consuming.*
- *I actively try to manage stress in my life, and I'm proud of the fact that I can do my job well and stay on an even keel most of the time. Maybe some people don't believe that a person can appear relaxed and handle this demanding job at the same time. But for me, maintaining my equilibrium is the key. It helps me function better and get things done more efficiently.*

### The "If It Ain't Broke" Argument
Emphasize the good work your team does, and remind the boss that she is thought to run a great department already.
- *This department is one of the best in the organization. We consistently get high ratings and extremely positive feedback from management and our customers. Why introduce a frantic pace when we are thriving at a normal pace?*

### Ask for Evidence
Ask your boss to cite an example in which your approach might have affected the quality of your work.
- *It's true that you and I don't necessarily handle things in quite the same way. After all, everybody's got a different style. But I do work hard and take my work very seriously. Have I done something recently that you thought wasn't up to par? Was there something I neglected? If so, I'd like to know about it so I can correct the problem.*

**Take Advantage of the Situation**

- *If you're concerned that the department doesn't appear to be keeping late enough hours, why don't we institute flextime? Some of us prefer an earlier schedule, and some would rather arrive and leave later. With flex hours, someone would be here covering things for a longer period every day.*

## When You're the Boss

For many people, the most dreaded workplace exchanges have nothing to do with standing up to the boss. Instead, they lose sleep over the prospect of having to issue a reprimand, critique inferior work, or deny someone's request for time off or a raise. They squirm and sweat when they have to say no to a subordinate.

Every manager is an authority figure to some degree, and that can be a two-edged sword. It's easy to enjoy the role when you get to play the "good cop." But if you're a boss who worries too much about being liked, you may actively avoid tough conversations. As a result, you'll probably find yourself putting up with sloppy work and situations that frustrate you.

To overcome managerial timidity, you must first acknowledge that *managing* is an essential part of your responsibilities. It comes with the territory, and if you run away from it, you're not doing your job. Think of it this way: When you offer constructive criticism and challenge employees to perform better, you're not just helping to make your own life easier. In the long run, you're also helping them to become more skilled, more valuable, and more employable. And you're helping your company do better, too.

Let's say you left your position tomorrow and a new manager came in to supervise your staff. Their odds of succeeding under the new regime will be much better if they've been encouraged to develop and excel. So if you're inclined to "protect" members of your staff by allowing standards to slide, you're not really doing them any favors.

"Okay," you may be thinking. "This all makes sense in theory. But I still dread the thought of telling someone that her work is unacceptable. What can I do?"

Keep the big picture in mind. Within the manager-employee relationship, as in many other situations, saying no or delivering criticism becomes easier for both parties when the overall context is a positive one. For the manager, that means taking advantage of every opportunity to praise good work and extra effort. Whether you do it face to face, by phone, memo, e-mail, or (best of all) in a meeting in front of others, it feels good to give people recognition for a job well done. And it also creates a more hospitable climate for those other times when you need to make constructive criticism or discuss below-average performance. By freely expressing your positive feedback at the appropriate times, you show that you're a fair person, not a negative one who only harps on flaws. Your "no" will be received better, and you'll feel less guilty about saying it.

## Saying No to Inferior Work

Do you often think, "I can do this faster/better myself"? It may seem easier in the short term, but when you find yourself regularly performing tasks that should be done by a subordinate, you're not saving time, you're misusing it. Wouldn't it be better if both of you could concentrate on doing the jobs you're being paid to do?

Ask yourself whether you're adding to your own burden in order to avoid confronting someone whose work is subpar. If so, it's only fair to both of you that you address the situation. Think of yourself as a teacher or mentor rather than a scold. Remember that you are in a position to help this person become more effective in his job and more valuable as a result. In order to do that, you need to make your expectations clear. 51

Rather than using negative words, focus on what needs to be done. Describe the goal. There's a big difference between saying, "This is a sloppy job; you're really careless," and "This needs to be more accurate. I want you to work on it some more and pay greater attention to detail."

**Critiquing a Particular Project**

Specify what can be done to improve the work, and challenge the employee to take responsibility.

- *I think your presentation could be a lot stronger in several areas. You need to add some solid research and organize your material better. Let's talk about that, and then I'd like you to work on it some more.*
- *This sales summary needs a lot more detail than you have here. I have to ask you to redo it, and this time be sure to include . . .*
- *Your time sheets are not as complete as I need them to be for our departmental review. Please take them back and add . . .*
- *I found four typos in your report, but I didn't mark them because it will be a good exercise for you to take it back and find them yourself. I want you to get into the habit of proofreading more carefully before you submit your work to me.*

**Saying, "This Is Your Job—Do It"**

- *I could do it myself, but if I did, you wouldn't ever develop the skills you need to perform your job. I need to be able to count on you. From now on, I want you to take full responsibility for this function.*
- *I've fallen into the bad habit of punching up your reports when I thought they were weak. But it would be fairer to both of us if you put more effort into them to begin with. After today I'm going to give them back to you when they need additional work.* (Be sure to indicate in specific terms what would improve the work.)

- *I know that keeping the supply room up to date and orga-nized isn't your favorite task. But it is part of your job, and it's an important function. The staff needs to be able to find things quickly when they're needed. I need you to make it a priority to keep that room in good shape.*
- *To do this job well, you need to bring in new business. Now, I know that making cold calls isn't everyone's cup of tea. But we are a sales organization, and that's one of the ways we prospect for new customers. Everyone in your po-sition is expected to make _____ prospecting calls per week. Can you tell me that in the future you will meet that goal?*

## Saying No to Requests from Employees

### For Time Off
- Prevention: Ask employees to give you as much advance warning as possible if they will need time off for personal business during regular working hours, so you can do what is needed to avoid conflicts. And let your staff know in advance when crunch times are expected, to discourage them from asking for time off when it's inconvenient.

If the timing's awful and you have to say no, stress the busi-ness reason for your decision.
- *With the regional managers' meeting coming up, I simply can't let you take vacation time before then. We've got a tremendous amount of material to produce, and we're al-ready behind schedule. I have to ask you to wait until after the meeting.*

Is there a way the employee can help you say yes? Ask her to solve the problem her absence will cause.
- *Friday is our busiest night, and we need a full staff working. But if you can find someone to fill in for you, I won't mind if you take off.*

- *This presentation needs to be shipped to the Frankfurt office tonight. If you can promise me you'll come back after your appointment and finish it up, I can give you a few hours this afternoon.*

### For a Raise or Promotion

Your power to reward a deserving employee may be quite limited by budgets and other factors beyond your control. While you must be honest about these limitations, you also have to satisfy the needs and expectations of the employee in some manner, assuming you don't want her to bolt out the door. She'll be gratified to know that you recognize her contributions and are looking for opportunities to reward her. But be careful—it's not fair to promise something you can't deliver.

- *You've made many contributions here, and I have to say you're an outstanding member of the team. You deserve to go further in the organization, and when the right opportunity opens up, I'll do what I can to help you advance. Right now I don't have a position to move you into. But things may change in the future. I can't promise anything, but if a more senior spot opens up that I feel you're right for, I will be in your corner.*

Even among valued staff members, not everyone is a superstar. Sometimes you need to adjust an employee's expectations to a more realistic level.

- *I'm sorry you're not happy with the increase you're getting this year. I hope you know how pleased I am with your work and how much I value your contributions. But other members of the department are contributing at a comparable level, and I need to be fair to everyone. The fact is, I'm given a limited amount of money for salary increases, and all the departmental raises come out of that pool. I wish I had more money to work with across the board. But under the circumstances, I think the raise I've given you is fair.*

At other times you'll want to say no because you don't feel the raise or promotion is justified. As much as possible, keep the focus on specific things the employee needs to do in order to improve performance and become eligible for the increase or change in title. If the position does not have clearly defined, stated goals, by all means develop some now. You need them in order to evaluate performance objectively.

- *I can't in good conscience authorize a salary increase until your performance is stronger than it has been. Let's look again at the goals for your position and talk about what you can do to become more effective. If you're willing to make a much greater effort over the next six months, you can become eligible for a raise at our next review period.*

- *Given your performance, I can't give you a raise at this time. Frankly, I see a lot of room for improvement. I want to help you make that happen, so let's talk about what needs to be done.*

- *Your performance is satisfactory, and I'm generally pleased with your work. But I'm not convinced that it merits giving you additional responsibility right now. Before I can recommend a promotion, I want to see you functioning at a truly outstanding level. If you're ready to make the effort, we can talk about what you can do to make yourself more promotable.*

Much as we love to "invoke the policy" to say no, in the workplace, saying "it's not our policy" makes you look (and feel) like a powerless bureaucrat. If that's what you are, try not to say it in so many words!

- *I understand you'd like a salary increase. Here at MegaCorp we deal with increases on a regular annual review basis. Raises are awarded based on standardized performance evaluations. After you've been here a year, we'll take a look at your progress and go from there.*

## "No's" from a Pro: Turning Down Job Applicants

Linda Wade is a human-resources professional whose responsibilities have included recruiting, compensation, benefits, and employee relations for a number of large corporations. Her work requires her to say no on a regular basis—which makes her something of an expert.

Following are Linda's guidelines for turning down prospective employees.

### 1. Be ready to explain.

"If I'm saying no to someone's job application, that person deserves to know why. It's not fair to leave people in the dark, where they could jump to all kinds of incorrect conclusions about why they were turned down.

"We recently interviewed a young man for an entry-level management position. Several managers he met with felt he wasn't well prepared for the interview, and they saw that as a bad sign. When I had to tell him that he didn't get the job, I said that while we all liked him personally (which was true), we felt he could have done his homework better before the interview. He asked for specific examples, which I was able to cite. Of course he was disappointed, but it was easier for him to accept our decision once he heard our reasons. We also gave him constructive feedback, which he may come to appreciate later."

### 2. Be kind.

"When it comes to hearing rejection, we're all sensitive. So I never forget the fact that I'm dealing with a human being who has personal issues and a background I know nothing about. Whenever possible I'll say something like 'It was a really close decision' or 'You have a lot to offer, but we found someone with a bit more experience or a couple more skills that we could use.' The fact is, you're giving them bad news, but if you're kind and compassionate about it, that goes a long way.

I always try to say something positive along with the 'no.' It's all in the translation."

### 3. Be clear.

"If you're too timid about saying no to someone, there's the danger that your message won't be understood. So when I'm having one of those difficult conversations, I make sure to include a phrase that conveys my meaning in very clear, unmistakable terms. For example, I'll explain our decision and then say, '. . . and on that basis, we are not going to continue the interview process.'

"It's a reality of my job that I have to tell people things they don't want to hear," says Linda. "But after twenty years in human resources, I know that the way you say it can make all the difference."

## When You're in Demand

In the quest for career success, you may feel pressured to say yes even when your instincts urge you to say no. Listen to your instincts.

### Saying No to a Job Offer

According to our friend Elaine, one of the hardest "no's" she has ever had to deliver was in response to a job offer.

"I was shocked by the amount of guilt I had when I had to turn down that job," she says. "I really choked over it."

It's flattering to be "courted" by a prospective employer who appreciates your talent and would love to get you on staff. Whose ego can't use a boost like that? It's also natural (and good career practice) to want to explore new opportunities and see what you might be worth on the open market. So you go to an interview, then maybe a second and a third one as well.

57

Sometimes people get swept up in the process and continue discussions even after deciding they're not going to accept the job. This was the case with Elaine. As she explains it, "I was torn between 'I don't want this to go any further' and 'Let's see how far this can go.' The job looked good on paper, and the salary was attractive, but I just wasn't getting the right vibe. My instincts told me not to take it. But I dreaded actually telling them."

It's easy to say that business is business, and a professional should be able to take a job refusal in stride. But if you happen to be a dyed-in-the-wool people-pleaser like Elaine, delivering news that you know will disappoint someone provokes major anxiety.

"I felt like a tease, like I'd gotten them all worked up and excited about hiring me and that by saying no I was going to leave them feeling betrayed and frustrated."

To let a would-be boss down easy, start by saying, *I've thought about this long and hard. It's a wonderful opportunity. But . . .*

- *After discussing it with you and your colleagues, I realize that the job isn't exactly what I'm looking for.*
- *This is not the right time in my life to take this job.*
- *The operation here is too lean for me to do the kind of job I'd like to do.*
- *I'm afraid I have to turn it down. My commitment to my current job/employer is stronger than I thought it was.*
- *I realize now that I can't take on the added responsibility in light of my already full schedule.*
- *I would not be able to sustain the time commitment and I wouldn't be able to give you a hundred percent.*

Before you turn the job down outright, consider whether you can parlay the offer into a work situation that suits you better. Perhaps you've been hoping to cut back, adopt a more flexible schedule, or take more frequent vacations and personal days. When there's an offer on the table, it may be the

## Top Job in the Country? I Don't *Think* So ...

. . . . . . . . . . . . . . . . . . . . . . . . . . . . . . . . . . . . . . . . . . . . . . . . . . . . . . . . . .

After bursting into the public consciousness during the Gulf War in 1991, Gen. Colin Powell quickly became one of America's most admired public figures. So it wasn't too much of a surprise when Republican political strategists launched a movement to draft Powell into the 1996 presidential race—despite the fact that no one seemed to know much about his politics. Poll after poll showed him ahead of all the other Republican candidates. It seemed as if the nomination, and quite possibly the presidency, were his for the asking—if only he wanted it.

Even when he said no, people didn't believe him, they were so accustomed to lying politicians and political motives for everything. But the general was neither a candidate nor a politician. He was a man who put his family and privacy ahead of other people's opinions of what he should be doing. We would do well to remember his example when we are feeling pressured to do something that is not on our own agenda.

ideal time to lobby not just for money but for whatever is valuable to you. If the position seems attractive but you're reluctant to make the commitment, why not try negotiating three days a week in the office and two days at home? It could pay off.

## Feast or Famine: Turning Down Business

Freelancers and other self-employed people often find themselves in a "feast or famine" situation: Either there's too much work or not enough. This knowledge can make it hard to control your appetite when there's an abundance of work on the table and it's all yours for the taking. But saying yes to more work than you can handle isn't good for business if you end up doing a sloppy job or blowing a deadline.

There's nothing wrong with saying no once in a while because you're really busy—it shows clients you're in demand. If you're gracious and helpful about it, you won't turn them away permanently. And don't be shy about asking prospective clients to call you the next time!

Here are some suggestions for saying no to a client when you're overbooked (or just want some time off).

- *Thank you for thinking of me. I'm afraid I'm spread a little too thin to take on another project now/this year/for some time to come. I wouldn't be able to give your project the attention it deserves. My calendar should open up around the first of November, so I hope you will call on me then if you need me.*

- *Thanks for calling me. I'd love to be able to help you out, but given my current workload I would be biting off more than I could chew if I said yes. I have enough work this month to keep me busy and then some. It's a mixed blessing, in that I love having the work, but I am sorry to have to say no to you. I'd really like to work with you, so I hope you'll let me take a rain check!*

### "May I Recommend ..."

Referring a customer to someone else is a generous thing to do, *and* it's good for business. By helping the customer and your colleague, you make yourself look good and generate positive feelings all around—which are bound to come back to you in the form of future work.

- *I'd love to work with you, but I'm afraid I'm already committed through the end of next month. However, I can recommend someone—she's a real pro, and I know she'll do a great job for you. (Give name and number.) I hope you will let me know how it works out.*

- *Thank you for asking me. I'm sorry that I have to turn down the chance to work with you. I'm not taking on any*

*new clients at this point. You might want to consult*
_____ *to find someone who is more available than I am.*
(Name a directory or other source where people in your
profession are listed.)

## Coping with the Rude, Offensive, and Illegal

There's one in every office—and if you're lucky, there's *only*
one. The guy who doesn't hesitate to tell you your ideas are
lousy. The woman who insults you via e-mail, with copies to
top management. The screamer. They make you want to
scream right back, or worse. But before you reach for the near-
est paperweight or other blunt instrument, take a step back.

Lashing out at a rude or offensive person will only cause
the problem to escalate and set a bad tone for your interactions in the future. Say no to obnoxious co-workers—including your boss, if necessary—by responding with a cool head
and insisting on civil behavior.

### Saying No to Rudeness

Your words will have more impact if you take the time to get
your emotions under control before speaking. Buy time by saying:

- *I can't discuss this with you if you're going to raise your
  voice to me/speak to me in that tone. Let's take a break and
  talk about this later, when we can speak to each other politely.*

#### Face It Head-On

When you're ready to talk, an in-person conversation is preferable to e-mail or a memo, which give your words a perma-
nence you may later come to regret. There's also no guarantee
your written communication will be kept private. Trying to
solve conflicts in writing is also problematic because it's too

easy to be misinterpreted. Tone is very important here. Once you're calm and collected, you'll be better able to convey your sincere interest in working things out if you speak to the person face to face and can see how your words are being received.

Remember that there may be two completely separate issues at hand: the rude behavior itself and whatever the situation was that prompted it. Don't let the rude person use the latter to justify the former.

- *I can put up with criticism, but I will not let you insult me/I will not stand for abuse. There is no reason to speak that way. If you have a problem, let's discuss it in a professional manner.*
- *I'm really trying to work with you here, but I don't feel that you're meeting me halfway. In the spirit of teamwork, can we put our emotions aside and look at the problem we have to solve?*

**"Acting Like a Jerk Is Bad for Business"**

Give the rude person a solid business reason that he shouldn't act like a jerk. Ideally, this will lead to a discussion on how you can work together more effectively in the future. It's important to show that you're willing to see the other person's point of view and compromise if necessary, but don't back down on your demand for courtesy. That's nonnegotiable.

- *You know, you have some really good ideas here. But sometimes they're hard to recognize because your manner can be so off-putting. When you make people angry, they don't want to like your ideas, so they look for reasons to reject them. I wonder if you realize the effect it has on people when you act rude to them.*
- *You're really defeating morale, mine and my department's. It's counterproductive, and it creates problems when we should all be looking for solutions. What can we do to improve this situation?*

## The Off-Color Office:
## Saying No to Sexual Harassment

Sexual harassment can take many forms and range from annoying to infuriating to extremely threatening. With all the surrounding publicity and ongoing national discussion of the subject in recent years, it's hard to believe that it still goes on, but of course it does.

The topic sparks so much heated debate because people continue to regard it in wildly subjective ways. Particularly in the workplace, one person's "compliment" can be heard as a highly inappropriate, vulgar remark, especially when colored by differences of rank. It's one thing when your boyfriend says you're a hot babe, but when your CEO says it, that's a different story.

There's simply no excuse for sexual harassment, so there's also no excuse to feel inhibited or guilty about blowing the whistle on this offensive behavior. That could mean blowing the whistle directly in someone's face and handling the situation yourself. It's up to you to decide whether to confront a harasser or make a complaint to a third party. Not everyone reacts with the same degree of outrage to sexual comments and gestures, and you may prefer to face down the offender yourself. (We're reminded of a rather blasé woman we knew in New York who, when a man exposed himself to her in public, rolled her eyes and said, "Oh, please, put it back in your pants, will you?") It all depends on the nature of the offense, your relationship, and your own personal makeup.

If you need third-party intervention, your human-resources department is the logical place to start. But if that option isn't available, contact a lawyer or the Equal Employment Opportunity Commission (EEOC). Check the U.S. government listings in your phone directory for the EEOC office in your region.

If someone is making you feel uncomfortable, degraded, or

threatened on the job, you can do something about it. Let harassers know that *you* know they're way out of line . . . and you don't intend to put up with it.

Here are some ways to say no to a harasser. They range in degree of intensity and cover a number of different situations.

### Keyword: "Inappropriate"

- *Don't. This isn't appropriate, I'm not interested, and I don't want this to go any further.*
- *That kind of talk is not appropriate in the office. It's offensive, and it makes me uncomfortable. Please stop.*
- *How dare you? That's totally inappropriate behavior, and I won't stand for it. Don't do it again.*

### The Loaded Hint

If "inappropriate" doesn't get through to this turkey, get tough by using loaded words like "harassment" or "formal complaint." Even a subtle suggestion that you might be litigation-minded can be a powerful deterrent.

- *I've tried to talk to you about this before, but apparently you didn't take me seriously. This feels like harassment to me.*
- *I've told you before that I think that kind of behavior/talk is out of line in the office. If I have to go to Human Resources with a formal complaint, I will.*

### "Where's Your Sense of Humor?"

A friend of ours witnessed the following scene in her office. Does it sound familiar?

An attractive female sales representative, who nearly always wore pantsuits, one day showed up at work wearing a rather short skirt. Before long, a crowd (all male) had gathered around her desk to remark on this momentous occasion. The mood was lighthearted, and a little "friendly" teasing ensued. One of the men—who just happened to be the head of the operation—said to the woman, "Stand up and show us your legs. We've never seen them before!"

Another chimed in, "What's the occasion, Janice? Is it because you finally shaved your legs?"

(We mentioned that this is a true story, didn't we?)

Janice, being the good sport that she is, laughed right along—even though a more fitting response would be something like "Buzz off, jerks." But because Janice is a realistic, practical gal who doesn't want to create bad blood with her boss or make trouble for herself on the job, she did what millions of women before her have done: She laughed it off.

You, however, may have trouble finding humor in this kind of situation if the teasing makes you feel angry and powerless. But within an unequal-power relationship, there are some subtle yet effective ways you can communicate the message that you object to out-of-line comments while still keeping the tone on the light side.

### The Raised-Eyebrow Treatment

For the following responses, act as if you're a little taken aback (not shocked—merely incredulous, as if to say, "Could somebody really be so foolish as to make a comment like that in this day and age? Doesn't he know he could get sued?"). Pull yourself up tall, raise an eyebrow, and say:

- *You didn't really mean to say that, did you?*
- (Direct this comment to a third party): *Did he say what I think he said? He didn't really say that, did he?*
- *Could you repeat what you just said?* (Keep asking him to repeat it several times.) *You really did say it, then, didn't you? I wasn't sure I'd heard right.*
- *Would you like to go out of the room and come back in so we can start this conversation over again?*
- *I'm surprised that you would ask me such a question. I'm going to do you a favor and pretend I didn't hear it.*

### Confidentially Speaking

Do you want to convey a little more seriousness? In a private conversation, imply that other people are offended, too, and that people are talking about it (but don't "name names").

- *You may not be aware of this, but some people were really taken aback by your comments. With the climate these days, you could get into trouble with that kind of talk. You never know what someone might complain about.*

### What Not to Say

Whatever you do, resist the temptation to counter sexist or sexual remarks by "harassing back." In other words, if you're greeted one day with a comment like "Nice sweater, Jane; what have you got in there—a couple of casaba melons?" resist the temptation to throw back an equally "clever" zinger like "What's that in your pants, Don—a Cheese Doodle?"

By engaging in this kind of banter, not only are you stooping to the harasser's idiotic level, you're allowing him to set the tone for all your future encounters. You're signaling that you're willing to play his game—and then you'll never hear the end of it. He'll probably take it as a compliment or a sign that you're interested in him. (Maybe you are—in which case, we have to ask, why? You can do better.)

Even if you enjoy the verbal jousting, these kinds of suggestive, off-color comments don't belong in the workplace. They may not bother you, but if they offend someone else, *that* can cause trouble for you. So don't abandon the moral high ground by trying to outharass a harasser.

## Other Harassment

Not all harassment is sexual. While it's unlikely that any co-workers will make offensive comments about your race or ethnic group in your presence, they may feel perfectly free to disparage other groups, thinking that you're of a similar mind.

Say no to this behavior, even though it's not directed at you. Many of the responses given above for sexual harassment can be adapted for other types of offensive remarks, and the procedure for lodging a formal complaint is the same. The more people tolerate "everyday" racism and prejudice, the easier it is for such attitudes to flourish. (See also "Stifle the Racist, Sexist Comments," page 130.)

## Saying No to Health or Safety Violations on the Job

Years ago Patti briefly held a job as PR director of a nightclub. One hour before the club's grand opening, she called the police to report that all the fire doors were chained closed from the inside, presumably to keep out crashers. Looking back, she wishes she'd had the nerve to confront her boss directly. Instead, she called the police anonymously. They arrived, inspected the premises, and corrected the problem before crowds arrived, averting a potentially dangerous situation.

If something on the job is putting you, your co-workers, or the public at risk, you have an obligation to bring it to the attention of someone with the authority to correct the problem. To say no to health and safety dangers in the workplace, report the problem to:

- *A representative within the company who has responsibility in that jurisdiction, e.g., your human-resources department.*
- *A union representative.*
- *Your state department of labor.*
- *OSHA (Occupational Safety and Health Agency), a division of the Department of Labor. Unless the situation is life-threatening, it may take quite a while for OSHA to respond to your complaint, so try other avenues first.*

## A Change for the Better:
## Saying No to the Status Quo

. . . . . . . . . . . . . . . . . . . . . . . . . . . . . . . . . . . . . . . . . . . . . .

Saying no in appropriate situations can gain you time, energy, and self-respect. But it's not enough to turn the wrong job into the right job.

Are you dying to say no to things you really can't say no to, because they're an essential part of your responsibilities? Do you work ridiculous hours because that's the nature of the business you're in? Does your work bore you or require you to betray a core value?

While you can't always pick and choose your dream job, you do have some control over whether the work you do meshes harmoniously with the life you want to live. We grow and change constantly; perhaps the job that suited you so well a few years ago doesn't fit anymore, because your priorities are different. Maybe now that you have a family, you hate spending half your time on the road. Maybe you've made some money and wish you had more time to enjoy it. Maybe you're just burned out and need some new inspiration in your life. It's time to move on to something more satisfying.

Saying no to an ill-fitting job is easy; the tough part, for most people, is knowing what to say yes to instead. That's a question everyone must answer for herself. (There are many good books that can help; we've listed a few in the Recommended Reading list, page 239.) Rather than requiring a major career change, it may simply be a matter of transferring your existing skills to a more pleasing situation. A nurse who's fed up with big-hospital bureaucracy might find greater satisfaction working for a private agency specializing in home care. A reluctant salesperson might be better suited to the role of buyer, working for one of the companies she currently sells to. An accountant who's soured on corporate life might be happier managing finances for a nonprofit organization.

It's important to consider your own temperament, too. Do
68 you prefer working alone or with lots of people? Do you want

a very challenging job or a relatively undemanding one that gives you lots of free time and flexibility? It's amazing to us how many people we've seen who were completely unsuited to their professions. We've known courtroom lawyers who hated to argue and debate, and elementary-school teachers who didn't like children. You've got to wonder whom they were trying to please by going into those fields, because they obviously weren't following their hearts.

To move toward more fulfilling work, it is first necessary to stop blaming your job and take responsibility for your own happiness. Sometimes the hardest part of a relationship is recognizing that you weren't really meant for each other. But if you can let it go, you'll leave the door open for something much better.

You don't *really* want to live a life of quiet desperation, do you?

## A Different Kind of Job Change

Many people who feel dissatisfied in their jobs enjoy the work itself but object to some other aspect of their employment, such as a rigid schedule, a long commute, or too-frequent business travel. If you're in that boat and yearning for a more balanced life, you may not need to bail out of your job altogether.

When we think of making a job change, it usually means moving from one job into another. But these days it could also mean changing the terms of the job you already have. With more and more employers adopting practices like flex hours, job-sharing, and telecommuting, there's never been a better time to negotiate with management. There may be an opportunity to redesign your current job so that it fits more smoothly into your life.

Unfortunately, we don't all work for forward-thinking companies. Some unenlightened employers—possibly yours—still regard these new practices as radical fringe experiments. But what have you got to lose by trying to usher them into the twenty-first century? If you do succeed in gaining even a little more flexibility, it might be just the relief you need to feel more in control of your life.

Talk to your immediate supervisor first, but if you don't get anywhere, consider putting a formal proposal in writing to a higher-ranking manager. The best way to get through to management is to speak in the language it understands: the language of business. Arm yourself with as much information as possible about companies that have introduced what are often referred to as family-friendly policies. Build your case with research and articles that attest to the bottom-line benefits for employers: reduced costs due to lower turnover; employees willing to go the extra mile because they're more motivated and committed to the company. *Business Week* magazine has conducted periodic surveys of work and family strategies among U.S. corporations and published articles that assess their impact on individuals and companies. *Working Mother* magazine's annual "100 Best Companies for Working Mothers" issue is another good place to find success stories (or if necessary, a better place to work!). A librarian can help you locate these resources as well as other research that supports your argument.

The early pioneers of the American West didn't always get to enjoy the fruits of their struggle, and maybe you won't either. But even if you don't see results during your tenure on the job, you'll be working for a good cause. That's something you can be proud of. And you never know—you might actually make an inroad or two.

## The Ultimate "No": Saying Yes to Self-Employment

One of the fastest-growing trends of recent years has been the large numbers of people who have left the corporate world to set up their own businesses, many of them home-based. Women are leading this movement toward self-employment. In a 1999 study, the Business Women's Network reported 8.5

million women-owned businesses in the United States, up from 6.4 million in 1992. Women are launching companies at twice the rate of men, and 51 percent of those with experience in the private sector cited a need for greater flexibility as their primary reason for going their own way.

Perhaps you've already thought about joining the ranks of these entrepreneurs, consultants, and freelancers who are striking out on their own. Both of the authors have traveled this path, and we're not looking back. Our postcorporate careers have allowed us to experience a freedom and sense of autonomy that would not have been possible otherwise. On the other hand, it's not for everyone. Self-employment is a risky, sometimes scary life, which requires a lot of hard work and self-discipline. If you can live with the unpredictable nature of self-employment—and if enough people are willing to pay for your products or services—it might be the right life for you, too.

Before making the leap, be sure to do plenty of homework to evaluate your market and develop a business plan. Talk to others in the field, scout out prospective clients, and look into some of the many books and on-line resources offering practical information and inspiration for those considering this route away from traditional nine-to-five life. (See the Recommended Reading list, page 239.)

## The Easiest Thing to Change: Your State of Mind

Maybe you've already made the decision to look for a new job or change careers. In the meantime, there's no need to suffer while waiting for your new life to begin. Even people who don't love their work can love what they're working *for*. It's possible to develop a whole new (and better) attitude toward your job by recognizing how it enables you to embrace what truly delights and inspires you.

You don't have to be rich to appreciate the things money makes possible in your life. Think of your paycheck as a re-

## Everyone Deserves a Little Bliss

Whether you work in a corporate office or a coal mine, there's nothing to stop you from taking your own path to a richer, more joyful life. Mythologist Joseph Campbell called it "following your bliss." Here are a couple of extracurricular ideas that might make you blissfully happy:

- *You never made it to Broadway, but you can join a community theater or a group that entertains in hospitals and nursing homes. (You will never find a more appreciative audience.)*
- *Your dream of becoming a veterinarian fizzled out sometime during tenth-grade biology. But if you love animals and want to be around them, you could volunteer at an animal shelter or get involved with an animal-rescue organization.*
- *Your dream of living in Tuscany is on hold while you raise a family and work fifty weeks out of the year. In the meantime, you can still experience* la dolce vita. *Take an Italian-language class, find people who share your interest, and plan Italian-themed cultural outings to films, museums, or restaurants.*

There may even be a way to make a living and indulge your passion at the same time. Some of the happiest people we know are embracing their dreams in these ways:

- *Ricki loves to travel, so she found a job in international sales that takes her all over the world on salary.*
- *Susie is a successful actress and singer. But even when times were lean, she stayed close to what she loved by working as a piano tuner and as assistant to a casting director. Both jobs gave her great contacts and a sense of accomplishment that have helped fuel her career.*
- *David is a musician, and between gigs he works in a music store. This puts him in contact with other musicians and students who want to study guitar with him. While working in a retail store was never his goal, his position keeps his dream alive and supports his musical career.*
- *Graham took a leave of absence from his corporate job to work as a sous-chef. The pay was terrible, the hours were worse, but he had*

> *a blast. Even though he went back to the office after one year, he*
> *was happy to have done something he always wanted to do and*
> *knew he would not spend the rest of his life wondering "what if?"*
>
> No matter what sort of bliss you crave, there's probably a group
> or organization devoted to it, a class you can take to get closer to it,
> and someone who'd really like to share it with you. Head to your pub-
> lic library, explore the Internet, look for information in newspapers and
> magazines that points toward the things you want to celebrate. Bliss is
> out there—go get it!

source to invest in your passions. The money you earn might allow you to care for your beautiful rose garden, play tennis on weekends, study French cooking, plan cultural outings with your children, or support an organization you've become involved with.

When you make time to enjoy things that make you feel happy and alive, your mood naturally improves. That's bound to carry over into the workplace, too. By channeling some of your earnings into pursuits and causes you feel passionate about, you'll be able to associate work with something that's special and meaningful, even if the actual work you do is neither. It's a more holistic approach to living: If you actively cultivate many sources of happiness, the worst job in the world won't seem quite so bad.

## Say No to Someone Else's Definition of Success

Our society defines success largely in terms of money and power. Since we want to be successful, it's easy to adopt the prevailing notion that the more money and power we have, the better. We then allow that belief to drive our lives. If we earn good money, we want to earn more money. The advertising industry exists to convince us we need more and more stuff. You've heard the slogan "He who dies with the most toys wins." We'd like to offer an alternative: "She who can best appreciate her toys wins."

In this culture, trading in a high-paying job for a less demanding one at a lower salary is still likely to raise some eyebrows. To opt out of the money chase is to swim against the tide. But tides change, and so do the times. Recent years have seen a growing movement of people who are rethinking the meaning of "success" and redefining it in their own terms. Today, if the relentless pursuit of cash leaves you feeling empty, it's good to know you have plenty of company—and other options.

### Recognizing "Enough": Saying No to Overconsumption

Probably the biggest reason people stay in jobs they hate is that they think they can't afford to live on less than they're earning. But there are plenty of people who have adjusted to smaller incomes and gone on to live as well as they had previously—sometimes even better.

How much *is* enough anyway?

Do you have enough food to eat for health and enjoyment? Enough clothing to keep you warm, cool, or appropriately attired for most occasions? A comfortable place to live, clean running water, heat on demand, air-conditioning, working toilets, a bed with clean sheets, a washer, dryer, dishwasher, a car? Most of these are luxuries to which a large portion of the world's population does not have access.

Before you take on that extra job or agree to handle one more client or accept that promotion that will require working longer hours for higher pay, consider whether the additional material goods you can buy will make your life any better than it already is. Will your quality of life really improve with one more impressive title? Money cannot add health, joy, love, or free time to our lives. Discretionary time, on the other hand, can often provide the temporary pleasures and deeper happiness that come from savoring our abundance and not always feeling rushed and pressured. Pay attention to whether you really do want to say yes when a chance for more money presents itself at the expense of your time. The continued pursuit of money after a certain comfort level has been achieved detracts from these more important goals for many of us.

Virtually all people who define themselves as middle-class could, if necessary, save significant amounts of money by making certain lifestyle changes and resisting knee-jerk consumerism. The simplicity movement that has emerged over the past few years has brought with it a number of excellent books on how to live a simpler, more meaningful life on a lot less money. One of the first and best is *Your Money or Your Life* by Joe Dominguez and Vicki Robin (see the Recommended Reading list, page 239).

Jumping off the money-chasing treadmill *is* a possible dream, and it's much easier when we learn to say no to some of the unimportant material items we've come to regard as necessities. People with a strong vision of what they want to say yes to are finding that the rewards make the trade-off worthwhile.

# Saying No to Invitations, Dates, and Romantic Entanglements

4

*You want lots of friends . . . but you also want to be left alone.*

*You're miffed if you're not invited . . . but you don't really want to go.*

*You want to have admirers . . . but considering some of the dates you've been on, you'd prefer to be admired from a distance.*

There's the dilemma of social life in a nutshell. On the one hand, as human beings, we crave connections with others. We like to be courted, to be invited to parties and included in the fun. On the other hand, we often find ourselves at social events wishing we were somewhere else instead.

## Saying No to Invitations

In theory at least, every invitation holds out the possibility of something delightful. "Come and play," it beckons. "You will sparkle/laugh/dance/feel warm/share/enjoy/find love/meet someone who can change your life." And sometimes, it happens. Parties *can* be fun, even magical. Where would Cinderella be if she hadn't gone to the ball? Too often, though, we know exactly what to expect—and it isn't magic. We've already seen the reality lurking behind that implied promise: another evening of superficial small talk and waiting for someone else to leave so we don't have to be the first. (The departure of that first guest so often sparks a mass exodus!)

Attending any social gathering requires a certain amount of time and effort—sometimes a great deal, depending on the circumstances. If it means you'll have to drive a long distance, hire a baby-sitter, or worry about what to wear, a so-so prospect becomes even less desirable. As an invitee, you have the right to consider whether the event justifies a "yes" response in light of the total investment you'll have to make in order to attend. What are the odds that you'll enjoy yourself enough to make it all worthwhile?

The time you have available to go to parties is the most precious time of all: those few hours left over after you've taken care of the "musts" like sleeping, working, commuting, obtaining and eating food, managing a household and family. For most of us, free hours are hard-won and too rare. That's all the more reason to spend them wisely.

Saying no to less-than-enticing invitations is one way to reclaim "golden hours" that might otherwise be lost in a whirl of busy-ness. Often we hear people express a desire to get out of a commitment they've already made. But wouldn't it be better if we could avoid making those commitments in the first place? Knowing when and how to decline invitations can help us find new sources of time to spend in a truly satisfying way— whether it's socializing more meaningfully with loved ones or seeking out a little much-needed solitude.

Our friend Leslie recently told us about a quiet evening she spent at home watching TV with her husband. Nothing special, right? It was to this couple. As working parents with two young children, relaxing together hasn't been an option at their house for the past several years. Finding themselves unexpectedly free to do nothing was a rare treat.

What you do with your newfound time is up to you. But first you must give yourself permission to claim it. Some people feel justified in turning down an invitation only if they've got something else on the calendar. But remember, "I've got plans" can mean many things, including plans with yourself to do nothing at all when you're longing for quiet time. If that makes you feel guilty, remember that what we in this culture call "vegging out" other cultures call "meditating" and take pretty seriously. With stress now widely recognized as a significant health hazard, there's something to be said for clearing out a little downtime to recharge your inner batteries.

Streamlining your crowded social calendar is an excellent place to start. This chapter offers a wide range of suggestions that can be applied to dozens of situations for declining invitations gracefully. Later on, we'll move into the romantic arena and discuss ways of turning down a date or putting the brakes on a relationship when you'd rather not move forward.

For all those times when you appreciate being asked but not the actual prospect of going . . . help is at hand.

## Knowing What Invitations to Turn Down

Before you accept an invitation to any event, stop to consider whether you really want to go. This would seem almost too obvious to mention, yet both of us have forgotten this important step on many occasions and paid the price for it later. Chances are you have, too. In the typical scenario, you're caught off guard by someone, respond to their invitation with a knee-jerk "yes," and commit yourself too fast. It might sound something like this:

> JACK: *Hi. Are you busy next Friday night?*
> YOU: *Let me see . . . no, I don't think so. Why?*
> JACK: *I'm having a little party after work. Can you come?*
> YOU: *Sure, I guess so.*

JACK: *Great! See you there! By the way, can you bring a few bags of chips and some salsa with you?*
YOU: *Uh . . . sure.*
[Fast forward to Friday, 5 P.M.]
YOU (thinking): *Oh, no! Jack's party! Chips and salsa! The supermarket at rush hour! A roomful of the same people I've been working with all week, rehashing the same old gripes! Cheap beer and cigarette smoke! Waaaaaaaa . . . I wanna go home!*

Socializing is not an exact science. In fact, the best, most fun times often seem like the opposite of science; they're spontaneous and unpredictable and can't necessarily be repeated. Chemistry, however, does play a big part. The best times happen when the right combination of people comes together at the right time under the right circumstances. You just don't know when it's all going to click. For this reason we encourage you to keep an open mind and consider each invitation carefully before responding. Saying no *too* easily could cause you to miss out on some very special, memorable times. Hermithood is not the end goal here. Sometimes you've just got to take a chance.

By knowing what kind of partygoer you are, however, you can usually predict pretty accurately whether the event in question will be your cup of tea.

- Do you thrive at large, crowded parties or hide out in the kitchen talking to one person all night?
- Do you enjoy "working the room" and meeting new people, or do you prefer more intimate gatherings with a select group of friends?
- Are you typically among the last to leave or the type who, twenty minutes after arrival, sidles up to your spouse or date and says, "Anytime you're ready . . ."?
- Will you scream if you have to attend one more baby shower this year?

Too often we don't ask ourselves these fundamental questions—or we do but don't listen to the answers. As a result, we end up at too many gatherings wondering, "What am I doing here? When does the fun start?"

## The Fundamentals

Just as the basic black dress is timeless and appropriate for so many occasions, so are the basic rules of graciously turning down an invitation or date. Here are our fundamental steps for saying no in social situations:

### 1. Buy Time

Many trusting souls have been trapped again and again by the trick question "What are you doing on \_\_\_\_\_?" Alternate forms of the trick question include "Are you free on \_\_\_\_\_?" or "Are you busy on \_\_\_\_?" and so on.

For the wise naysayer, there are only two proper responses to this question:

A. "I have plans. Why?"

or

B. "I think I have plans. Why?"

When asked a blind question like "What are you doing Saturday?" you have no way of knowing whether you're about to be invited to a barbecue or to help move a grand piano up a flight of stairs. Answering "I have plans" prevents you from being forced into an uncomfortable position with no means of escape. It does *not* mean you're saying no automatically. You're merely buying time to consider your options carefully without undue pressure.

Once you hear the invitation, if you decide you'd really like to go, it's easy enough to "rearrange your schedule" and say yes. The person doing the inviting will probably be very pleased that you're enthusiastic enough to change your plans.

But don't rush to respond. As the following dialogue shows, sometimes *full* knowledge is power:

FRIEND: *What are you doing Saturday night?*
YOU: *I have plans, why?*
FRIEND: *We've got tickets to see* Les Misérables *on Broadway and . . .*
YOU: *Great! I'll rearrange my plans!*
FRIEND: *. . . and we wanted you to baby-sit.*
YOU (thinking): *Damn!*

### 2. Appreciate Being Asked

Whether or not you're inclined to attend a particular event, it's important to remember that invitations mean someone desires your company. Usually it's not the *person* you want to say no to but the event itself, or its timing, location, or some other factor. Even if you don't go, enjoy the fact that you've been invited, and be generous in your thanks to the host. Let him or her know how much you appreciate being included, and savor the good feeling you get from that knowledge. When you can sincerely say, "I'm so glad you thought of me," your warm feelings will come across even while explaining that you can't attend. As in many other situations, saying no to an invitation is much easier for all parties when the overall context is a positive one.

### 3. Respect Your Prior Plans—Even If They're with Yourself

Refuse to feel guilty about turning down invitations in order to give yourself some personal time. While relationships with others are vitally important to most of us, this doesn't mean that time spent with others is always superior to time spent alone. Not all interaction is fun or meaningful. At times your spirit requires something other than a cocktail party. Nurture your relationships, absolutely. But honor your commitments to yourself as well.

### 4. When in Doubt, Say No

If you're waffling about whether to attend a particular event, "no" is the more flexible option. Unless it's a catered affair such as a wedding, most hosts will be delighted if you change your mind late in the game and ask to attend. Saying, "My plans fell through; is the invitation still open?" is far preferable to canceling on the day of the event.

### 5. Consider Honesty

Before you make excuses, think about whether they are even necessary. Sometimes excuses can backfire.

Our friend Lucy recently told us about an incident that brings this to mind. On the day her book-discussion group was scheduled to meet, Lucy got a call from another member of the group. The caller explained that she wouldn't be able to attend that night and launched into a breathless, complicated story: Her husband had been suddenly called away to Asia on business, she needed to pack his bags for him and meet him at the airport with his passport, and the kids were scattered in different locations all over town and how was she going to pick them all up in time? Well, it was clear she couldn't make the meeting.

The only thing is, later that day Lucy stopped off at her town's public pool for a swim, and who did she see there? The woman's husband, relaxing in his bathing suit and showing no signs of being en route to Asia.

Was his wife a pathological liar? Or did she feel that the only way she could back out of her book-discussion meeting was if she had an elaborate excuse? Either way, her lies caused a rift in her relationship with the other members of the group, who felt betrayed that she didn't level with them. Says Lucy, "If she had simply called and said, 'I'm not up to it tonight,' it would have been no big deal. We're all friends; we would understand. The fact that she felt she had to make up a big phony story shows me she doesn't respect us or trust us. And now we don't trust her."

Which points to another good reason to make lying the choice of last resort: You could get caught, and dishonesty is very bad for relationships.

## The Answering Machine: Your Best Friend

Do you ever get calls from people who just happen to be in the neighborhood and want to drop by? Routinely screening your calls puts power back into your hands, allowing you to avoid unwanted spur-of-the-moment invitations or buy time before responding in other situations. Not only does it control interruptions at home, it protects you from people who might be calling to invite you to their vacation slide show.

Use answering machines to say no for you. When you want to decline an invitation but don't want to get involved in small talk or a long conversation, save time by calling when you know the other person won't be there. Express your regrets on the answering machine.

## Invited Versus Expected: Recognize the Difference

Ask any veteran party-giver, and she'll tell you her opinion of people who agree to attend but then don't show up. (Hint: It isn't good.) Please don't be one of these people. There's a big difference between being invited (when there's still a choice to make) and being expected (when you've already accepted). We're not talking about legitimate cancellations due to illness or emergency. We're talking about people who say yes to invitations because they're afraid to say no and want to be "nice." Or because they're not sure how they'll feel that day and want to leave their options open.

The worst example is a person who fails to take seriously a commitment to attend a wedding or other expensive function. If your hosts are planning to spend a considerable amount of money to feed and entertain you, the least you can do is honor them with your presence. Make sure it's not *your* name on one of those little place cards left conspicuously standing after all the other guests have arrived and found their tables. Otherwise, you're liable to be crossed off the guest list forever—with good reason.

## Saying No to Parties, Dinners, and Other Social Engagements

(For weddings and other family functions, see page 117.)

### Buy Time
Unless you're prepared with a definitive, absolute "no," buy time to think about your response.

- *It sounds great! Let me check my calendar, and I'll get back to you.*
- *What fun! I'll have to check with my husband/wife/partner to make sure we don't have anything else lined up for that day.*
- *I'm pretty sure I have something else that night. Let me check and get back to you.*
- *Sounds like a lot of fun! I hope I can get a baby-sitter. I'll let you know.*

### Keep It Simple
In the process of turning down an invitation or date, we often have a tendency to babble on and make excuses. But it may not be necessary. Why not experiment with a "minimalist" approach? You may be pleasantly surprised at how simple it is (and you won't have to lie).

- *What a great invitation! I wish I were free that weekend.*
- *I wish I could. It sounds terrific. Unfortunately, I have other plans.*
- *I'm sorry, I'm busy. I wish I had time to come.*
- *I had such a good time at last year's party. I'm sorry I can't make it this year. (Optional: Supply details of last party, e.g., "Remember when Jack got drunk and fell in the pool?")*
- *I'm afraid I can't make it, but I'd love to see you. Can we*

*make a date for the two of us to get together for dinner the week after?*

## Saying No to the Nosy

Not everyone will accept your refusal graciously. There will be those who just can't take no (or "I have other plans") for an answer and insist on knowing what you're doing instead. You may feel that making up an excuse is your only recourse (see "Last Resort: Face-Saving Excuses," page 86). If you'd rather keep it vague, tell them, "Frankly, it's personal." That should persuade all but the rudest people to drop the subject. And why indulge *them?*

## Honest Excuses

In some situations, being perfectly honest is the best way to turn down an invitation. Taking the other person into your confidence is a gesture of trust that can establish a bond of understanding between the two of you.

With any of the following responses, it helps to begin by saying something like *I'm going to be honest with you because I know you'll understand.*

- *I need the downtime.*
- *I've had houseguests all week, and I really need some time to myself.*
- *I'm just exhausted, and I wouldn't be much fun.*
- *I really need a break from parties and crowds of people. Let's get together in a few weeks when things calm down.*
- *On another day I would say yes in a minute. But today's been a rough day, and I need to go home.*
- *I'd like to meet your friends, but I wouldn't be good company tonight.*

The big potential drawback of being honest is that a friend who feels you don't "technically" have an excuse may try hard to talk you into coming. Be prepared for this, and don't be swayed if the person persists; just repeat what you've already

said about needing some time off. If necessary, use a little pressure of your own.
- *You know, pressuring me isn't going to help.*
- *I gave you an honest answer because I thought you'd understand.*

### Last Resort: Face-Saving Excuses

When all else fails, you may need to come up with a good excuse. While as a rule we don't encourage lying, it does occasionally come in handy for preserving relationships. Face-Saving Excuses are preferable to brutal honesty that would hurt someone or cause a rift in a friendship (*Dinner at your house? Oh, no, I hate your cooking*). When a less-than-truthful response seems to be the only way out, it's best to keep your excuse simple. Supplying too many fictional details makes it easier to get caught in a lie, as the earlier story about the woman in the reading group illustrates. The classic alibis work best and are less likely to be questioned: kids, relatives, pets, and work.

Blame the children.
- *One of the kids hasn't been himself lately, and I want to keep a close eye on him.*
- *We have yet to find a baby-sitter we can trust with our kids.*
- *I can't get a baby-sitter on such short notice.*

Blame the family.
- *My husband/wife/partner already committed us to something that night.*
- *We have a family wedding to go to.*
- *I promised my sister I would baby-sit for her kids that night.*
- *My in-laws are coming to town, and we promised to spend some time with them.*

Blame the pets.
- *I have to go home and walk my dog.*
- *I have to go home and feed the cats.*
- *I have to take my bird to the vet.*
- *I have to take my dog to the groomer; it took me months to get an appointment.*

Blame work.
- *I can't. I'm on deadline.*
- *I'll be working late that night.*
- *It's our busy season, and I've got to be on call.*
- *It's my husband's busy season, and I need to be available to watch the kids if he has to work.*

Blame extracurricular activities.
- *I have a PTA meeting.*
- *I've got a class that night. (Be prepared to say what the class is.)*
- *I've got a reunion with old friends, and you know how hard it is to coordinate those things.*
- *I have to wait for the plumber.*

Use excuses like these with caution. The lovely thing about honesty is that you don't have to remember which cockamamie story you told to which person. So if you declined a date by saying you had to go to a wedding, don't get caught at Kmart shopping for hamburger buns.

## Command Performances:
## When "No" Isn't Really an Option

Beware the seemingly optional event that isn't. This applies to business-related social functions and certain family events in particular. At times when attendance might not be "officially" mandatory, your absence might be noticed, and there could be consequences. So if the CEO of your company invites you to a cocktail party to introduce the board of directors, you'd better make every attempt to be there. Recognize when "Be there if you can" really means "Be there or else." Some invitations are really obligations. Ignore them at your own risk.

## The Unsuitable Suitor: Saying No to Dates and Romantic Entanglements

Here's where it gets a little more difficult.

Turning down invitations in general requires a certain amount of finesse. But when an invitation carries the potential for romance, things can really get tricky. Saying no to a date—whether it's the first, second, or tenth—has more personal implications than, say, declining an invitation to your cousin's dinner party. Instead of just being about one evening or one event, this "no" communicates something about the entire relationship, usually that you don't want it to continue, at least on the terms the other person is hoping for.

When it comes to personal attractiveness and desirability, we're all pretty vulnerable. For someone who's sensitive to the feelings of others (which you probably are, since you're reading this book), being the "rejecter" can be as hard as being the "rejectee." Often it will bring up some old hurt of our own. Because we remember all too well what it felt like, we dread the prospect of inflicting pain on another person. As a result, we can really lose sleep figuring out how to say no.

But shying away from the inevitable is unfair to both of you. When you don't want to date someone or move a relationship forward, it only complicates matters to send mixed signals or encourage false hopes. You can reduce the likelihood of causing painful injury by learning some useful techniques for saying no and letting someone down gently.

While kindness is a worthwhile goal, keep in mind that this is no time to be vague and ambiguous. Unless you communicate clearly, you run the risk that your message won't get through at all, and then you'll be right back where you started. Like it or not, a certain amount of disappointment is necessary. Our favorite observation on the subject comes from Miss Manners, a.k.a. Judith Martin. In her book *Miss Manners' Basic Training: The Right Thing to Say,* she reminds us of the simple fact that "a person who doesn't feel rejected doesn't go away."

The sooner you speak up and say no to an unsuitable suitor, the sooner you can both move on.

In case you think we're encouraging you to avoid dating, isolate yourself, and live like a monk, think again. We're well aware that happy relationships start with dates, and no one ever found love by hiding out at home under the bed.

## Know What You're Looking For

Why is it so important to cut down on unsuitable suitors and unsatisfying relationships or, better yet, avoid them in the first place? One obvious reason is to save yourself from the occasional unpleasant evening. But there is a deeper purpose involved: so that you can devote your energy to finding a partner who *will* fill your needs and so you can create more opportunities to pursue your vision of the person you want to say yes to. (If you're asking, "What vision?" we'll get to that in a minute.) It's not simply about claiming more free time, though that's part of it. It's also about how you use that time, what you might be doing and thinking if you weren't stuck there struggling to make conversation with Mr. Wrong or Ms. Stake.

When you consider a romantic prospect and decide, "This is not what I want" or "This isn't what I'm looking for," you take a step away from something. But in the meantime, do you know what you are going *toward?* Unless we know what we are looking for, we're left standing at the crossroads with no idea of which direction to take. Without a destination in mind, we're liable to get on any old bus that comes down the road—and who knows where it may be headed?

Think of it this way: If you're looking for someone you've never met, it helps to have a description or a picture of the person you're looking for. That's where the "vision thing" comes in. In the context of love and romance, it means having a clear mental picture of the person you want to meet and keeping that picture in your mind as you go through the process of meeting, dating, and relating. We're not talking about your fantasy lover's looks. We're talking about *essence*. Develop your picture by focusing on the qualities in a romantic partner that are absolutely essential to you. They may include things like kindness, a sense of humor, attractiveness, and generosity. Concentrate on the "nonnegotiable" traits that are truly necessary for you to have a happy relationship. Others, such as being a good dancer, may be appealing but less important in the long run.

## Attracting What's in Your Mind

A number of ancient-wisdom traditions, as well as many contemporary spiritual teachers, have put forth the idea that by visualizing something in a conscious, purposeful way, you will find it more easily—and it will find you. This is also the basic premise of Shakti Gawain's inspiring book *Creative Visualization*, an extremely useful guide to the practice.

The reasoning is that when you invest a lot of energy thinking about something, you will attract it into your life. What you concentrate and focus on will come to you. Each of us sees the world through our own lens. When we create and maintain a vision in our minds, we begin to see it outside of ourselves.

Does this sound like fantasy? Then consider it another way. We've all known people who are perpetually angry at the world. They're always imagining slights when none were intended and are often heard complaining about others. In stores and restaurants, they're the first to gripe about bad service. Is it just an accident that of everyone we know, these people get into more fights and encounter incompetent fools every day of their lives?

Of course not. It's because their vision of the world is colored by the vision in their heads. Because they bring hostility to every encounter, they encounter hostility everywhere.

The opposite is just as true. People who are optimistic and friendly attract other friendly people. Meeting the same set of people as the angry fellow, they'd find everyone perfectly pleasant instead. They're seeing their own state of mind reflected in the people they meet. Are they just "seeing what they want to see"? Absolutely, and that's exactly the point. In the process, they're also *attracting* what they want to see—warmth and friendliness—because most of us are drawn to warm, friendly people. Aren't you?

Patti firmly believes that visualization enabled her to meet her husband, Stan. She told herself every day, "I'm in love with a kind, smart, generous, happy, healthy man who loves me." Day after day, the image began to seem more real, and the "fantasy" began to seem more and more possible. Her point of view shifted; instead of wondering, "Does he even exist?" she now told herself, "He's out there. It's only a matter of finding him."

She then placed a personal ad in a local newspaper, which drew many responses, including one from her future husband. Ironically, Stan almost didn't "make the cut," because he failed to meet two of the criteria Patti had listed in her ad. He lived too far away and was more than ten years older than she. Luckily, he was convinced of their potential together and persuaded her that geography and age were relatively minor in the grand scheme of things. (They are. Anyone can move . . . or be young at heart). As she got to know Stan, she saw that the traits she valued most were present in abundance. Once she found someone who was compassionate, smart, and funny, the other stuff just didn't seem to matter very much.

## Use Dates as a Learning Laboratory

Saying no becomes easier when you know what you want to say yes to. To help yourself zero in on what that is, use the experience of dating as a laboratory for exploration and study.

Each time you say no, it's because you've recognized something you don't want or something you do want that's missing. With every date, you can tell yourself that you're getting closer and closer to finding someone who really excites you and feels right for you.

Even unsuccessful dates can help sharpen your vision and focus on the qualities in a partner that attract and delight you. Make it a practice to look for something to like about everyone you go out with. Maybe one is a good dresser but has terrible table manners. Another may be friendly and warm but unable to talk about anything but sports. To help yourself get through the evening, focus on what you do like about the person and keep those attractive qualities in mind. If nothing else, it makes the dating process more fun. But it's also rewarding to develop the habit of finding things to appreciate in other people. It's not necessary to add all these "positives" to your list of nonnegotiable requirements. But by consciously looking for things to admire in others, you're training yourself to zero in on a person's best qualities faster.

Seeking out your life partner is like trying on clothes in a department store. When the outfit clicks, you know it works because you tried on all those others that didn't work. For example, when you know you look terrible in red, you don't need to bother trying on red dresses. The date who is rude to the waitress is showing his colors, too, and nobody says you have to like them. Don't settle—say no and keep shopping.

## The First Date . . . and Saying No

To go or not to go? Even though one of our basics for invitations is "when in doubt, say no," the dating arena is a little different. It calls for a willingness to experiment. Giving someone the benefit of the doubt could have unexpectedly happy results. You might have a much better time than you thought or see a new side to the person that surprises you in a very pleasant way. If you're truly on the fence about whether to accept a date, we say go for it.

Even if it doesn't work out, saying yes to dates offers other benefits. Like going on job interviews, dating gives you a chance to practice your "skills." The more often you do it, the more poised and comfortable you become with the whole process. Going on dates also helps expand your network. While the two of you might not hit it off romantically, you could become friends, and friends are still the best way to meet other really, really *good* friends! The wider your circle, the more opportunities you will have to meet someone who's just right for you.

Sometimes, however, there are no doubts to wrestle with. You just need to say no. The best approach is to keep it short. Don't invite debate by overexplaining the reasons for your "no." If the unsuitable suitor doesn't take no for an answer, keep to your point. Many of the responses below can be used in combination with each other and can be repeated until your message sinks in. Don't get trapped into having to justify yourself.

When turning down dates or curtailing a relationship, keep the focus on yourself by using "I/me" language (e.g., "*I'm* not ready to get involved" or "This doesn't feel right to *me*"). This avoids suggesting that the other person is inadequate in some way and seems less like personal criticism.

Because people tend to hear what they want to hear, it's important to make your intentions crystal clear. Always begin with an unequivocal statement such as *I'd rather not . . .* or *No, thank you . . .* that can be combined with one of the responses below.

(If you find this kind of "no" especially difficult to say, it may help to practice these responses out loud first or even role-play with a friend.)

### Gentle Letdowns

- *I don't want to take our friendship in that direction.*
- *I'm not eligible right now.* (This covers many situations.)
- *That's not what I'm looking for.*
- *I'm not in a dating mode right now.*
- *I just started seeing someone.* (Regardless of the outcome from your last date with someone else, imply that you're already involved elsewhere.)
- *No, you remind me too much of my ex.*
- *I'm still hoping to get back together with my ex. I don't want to start any new relationships until that's resolved.*
- *My heart and mind are with somebody else.* (This could refer to someone you haven't met yet.)
- *It would never work.* (Why?) *It just wouldn't. I know.* (But why?) *I have a strong feeling about it.*

### The Policy

Think about whether you can turn down this date by invoking a policy, such as:

- *I don't date guys from work.*
- *I don't date guys who aren't my religion.*
- *I don't date guys who used to be married to my mother.*

But don't abuse the Policy excuse. For example, "I don't date guys named Kevin" is not an appropriate response.

### The Classic

It worked for your mother and grandmother; it will work for you, too:

- *I'd like us to be just friends.*

### Truly "Just Friends"

When you really *would* like to be "just friends," here's a way of expanding your network and increasing dating opportunities for both of you:

- *I don't want to take our friendship in that direction. But I'm planning a party with some of my friends. Why don't you bring some of your friends and come along?*

### No Dating Within the Group

If you're part of an ongoing group, such as a bicycling club or bowling league, and another member asks you out, you can say no by telling the person that you'd feel awkward about mixing dating with another activity you really enjoy.

- *Bird-watching is really important to me. I want to keep enjoying it. I'd feel uncomfortable if we went on a date and it didn't work out. I'd rather not have that kind of involvement with someone from the group.*
- *I don't want to add the anxiety of dating to the pleasure I get from being part of the rock-climbing club. It would change my whole relationship to the group.*

### No Time

Sometimes life feels so overwhelming that you truly don't have the time or energy for dating. If so, don't be afraid to say it.

- *I don't have room in my life for this right now.*
- *I have too many distractions. I wouldn't have time to focus on dating right now.*

## Saying No to Second and Subsequent Dates

Good for you—you gave it a chance and went on that first date. And while it wasn't gut-wrenchingly awful, neither was it an experience you care to repeat. At this point, if it feels all wrong, it's wise to listen to your instincts. When a second date is among the least appealing prospects you can think of, nip it in the bud. In addition to the following "no" responses, many of those listed above will work here as well.

When he or she asks, "Can I see you again?" say, "I have to be honest with you," and add any of these:

## Dress Rehearsal: Practice with Personal Ads and the Internet

. . . . . . . . . . . . . . . . . . . . . . . . . . . . . . . . . . . . . . . . . . . . . . . . . . . . . . . . .

Dating can be an anxiety-fraught activity, especially if you're someone who has extreme difficulty turning down dates or saying no to unappealing relationships. Here's a technique that can help raise your comfort level with the whole process.

Practice your naysaying skills by taking out a newspaper or an on-line personal ad, with the full intention of saying no to everyone who responds. Resolve to speak with at least five prospects over the phone, but don't meet anyone in person. At the end of your conversation, say, "It's been nice chatting with you, but I don't think this is what I'm looking for." Or use one of the other responses we've provided in this chapter. It's a no-sweat, no-commitment way to get used to saying no when there's very little at stake. Also, it's easier to be bold and to practice saying no when you can remain anonymous.

Of course, if the person on the phone sounds absolutely irresistible, feel free to toss the no-meeting policy out the window!

- *This isn't working for me.*
- *I think this is not meant to be.*
- *I don't think we should see each other anymore.*
- *I've enjoyed spending time with you, but this doesn't feel right to me.*
- *I've enjoyed getting to know you, but I just don't think it's in the stars for us.*
- *I'm not comfortable with us being together.*
- *Seeing you made me realize I'm not over my ex yet* (or: *I'm not ready to date again yet*).
- *Seeing you made me realize that my heart and mind are with somebody else.*
- *I have some serious issues that I'm working through. So this isn't the right time for me.*

- *I'm surprised you're asking; I didn't think we had the right chemistry.*

### Leaving Your Options Open

Sometimes you may want to create some distance without closing the door entirely.

- *Let's not rush into this. I need some space.*
- *Let me think about that. Maybe I'll call you.* (A lot of people—okay, a lot of men—have gotten away with saying, "I'll call you," as a way of saying good-bye. By adding a "maybe" to that famous line, you're sending a strong "No, thanks" signal.)

### Don't Elaborate

For some peculiar reason, many people insist on hearing the gory details about why you don't want to see them anymore. Don't give in to them. Choose kindness over full disclosure and you'll both be happier in the long run. If he or she presses you for specifics, hold your ground.

- *I don't feel I need to elaborate.*
- *I have nothing more to say about it.*
- *Enough said.*
- *I just don't want to continue, and that's all there is to say. Please don't ask me anymore.*

## Saying No to Unwanted Sex

Sex is a great and powerful force, but if the circumstances aren't right, it can be powerfully awful. It's important to be able to assert yourself if things seem to be moving along faster or further than you're comfortable with.

In the course of a relationship, it often happens that one person arrives at the "I'm ready!" stage way ahead of the other person. John Gray's book *Mars and Venus on a Date* explores the different stages of dating and looks at why it's important not to rush into the intimacy stage if you're looking to build a lasting relationship. The book's insights can help you recognize whether the time is right to make it sexual and how to negotiate with a partner who might have other ideas.

When it comes to sex, people often have trouble expressing their desires (or lack of desire). Suggestions follow.

### Prevention

A young woman we know let a man of her acquaintance whisk her off to a luxurious Caribbean resort for the weekend. On arrival, she was shocked—shocked!—to learn he had reserved only one room for the two of them. Silly girl.

At the risk of sounding like your mother, we must remind you that the Absolute, Number One, All-Time Best Defense Against Unwanted Sexual Advances is to avoid those situations where they're likely to happen. In other words, if you're not open to a sexual encounter, don't meet him at his house, apartment, or hotel room, and don't invite him to yours. That's what restaurants, bars, and hotel lobbies are for. Prevention is less awkward than having to fend off his unwelcome attentions—and safer.

### "Not Yet"

- *This is too soon. I'm not ready for this yet.*
- *I'd like to get to know you better first.*
- *Our relationship needs to develop more before I'll be ready for that.*
- *I don't want to rush things.*
- *I think we should go out a few more times before we jump into bed.*
- *Until I feel like we've had enough romance I'm certainly not interested in sex.*

### "Never"

- *That's not what I want from this relationship.*
- *I'm not interested in having that kind of relationship with you.*

- *I've made a decision to not have sex until I'm married.*
- *If that's what you're after, you'd better find someone else.*

### When More Forceful Language Is Needed
- *Guess what? I think I might have a venereal disease.* (We know someone who used this line successfully to get out of a rather intimidating situation.)

## Saying No to Unsafe Sex

Don't fool around with this one. The potential for contracting sexually transmitted diseases, including HIV, is all too real, and the consequences are much too serious. Male or female, all sexually active people must be responsible for protecting themselves, so it's smart to carry condoms with you even if you don't expect to use them.

Another important way to protect yourself is to anticipate how you will address the issue with a partner *before* you find yourselves in the heat of passion. If you think it will be especially hard to talk about this, practice saying these responses out loud first:

- The Policy: *I have a strict policy about using condoms. Do you have one handy? If not, I do.*
- *Safe sex is the only kind of sex I have.*
- *Hold on a minute . . . I have a condom in my bag. Let me get it.*
- *Do you have a condom?* (If yes): *Let's use it, please.* (If no): *Then let's postpone this until you get some.*

If your partner objects, try one of these:
- *This is a nonnegotiable demand.*
- *It's too serious to fool around with.*
- *You may be frustrated now, but you'll thank me in the morning.*
- *Good-bye. I've got to go.*

## Saying No to Guilty Sex

Ah, sex and guilt. Are they destined to overlap forever?

We all know the traditional type of sex-related guilt. It strikes people who believe that premarital, extramarital, homosexual, or "creative" sex is sinful, yet they go ahead and do it anyway because their passions get the better of them.

But there's another kind of sexual guilt. That's when you go ahead and have sex with someone because you'd feel guilty if you *didn't*. Instead of sex-related guilt, it's more accurate to call it guilt-related sex.

How does it happen? Let's say there's a man who's gone gaga over you. He's sent you flowers every day this week. Tonight he took you out to a fabulous restaurant and then to the hit show you've been dying to see. The guy's obviously smitten. And while you're not too keen on the idea of jumping into bed, he just makes you feel so . . . *grateful.*

The man who showers you with expensive gifts may be a perfectly nice fellow with the best of intentions. We don't know him, so we can't say for sure. But it's a pretty safe bet that whoever he is, he *does* want to get you into bed. His eager courting could effectively pressure you into something you're not ready for (or may never be enthusiastic about). No matter how good a time you've had and how much money was spent, you don't owe him anything except a sincere thank-you. The rest is optional.

If you're bothered by the feeling that you're taking too much and not giving enough, there are other ways to balance things out besides using sex as a way to say thank you. The simplest: Accept fewer gifts, and pick up the check yourself once in a while. With that in mind, here are some ways to say no (indirectly) to guilt-related sex:

- *The necklace is beautiful, but I can't accept it. I'd feel too indebted to you, and that's not what I want this relationship to be about.*
- *It's so thoughtful, but I don't want you to give me such an*

*expensive gift so soon in our relationship. If we're still going strong a year from now, you can give it to me then.*

- *I'd love to go—but I insist we go Dutch this time. I wouldn't be comfortable otherwise.*
- *The concert sounds great, as long as you let me take you out to dinner afterward.*
- *A mink? I appreciate the thought, Henry, but I wouldn't be caught dead wearing fur!*

## Saying No to a Longer-Term Relationship

Once you've moved beyond dating into the "boyfriend/ girlfriend" stage, you've probably invested a good deal of time and emotional energy in the relationship. It stands to reason that a longer-term bond will be more difficult to break. By now you've got a history and memories.

Where once you might have had high hopes for a future together, perhaps you've come to realize that the two of you are on different wavelengths. Your expectations aren't the same; things aren't going in the direction you want them to go. Or maybe you've finally acknowledged that this person is not going to fulfill your needs in the long run.

Whatever your reasons for wanting to say "no more," there's no denying that breaking up is hard to do. Lana Staheli, Ph.D., author of *"Affair-Proof" Your Marriage*, has counseled many people through break-ups. "There's no way for it not to be painful," she says. "You're going to feel bad, your partner's going to feel bad. But people make the mistake of thinking, 'If I'm having all these feelings, that must mean it shouldn't have ended.'"

One of the best ways to strengthen your resolve to end a relationship that isn't working, says Dr. Staheli, is to remember what it is you *do* want and to focus on moving forward. "You will miss this person. You'll recall the good times. There are times you'll even think about being back together. That doesn't mean it's a good idea."

How *do* you cut it off? Unlike most of the situations we address in this book, saying no to a serious relationship is generally a process rather than a single event. "There's back-and-forth; it's usually part of a discussion that happens over a period of time," says Dr. Staheli. Nevertheless, she advises using many of the same techniques we recommend for saying no to first and second dates: "Be repetitive rather than trying to come up with new reasons. It's fine to simply say, 'This doesn't work for me,' or 'I can't continue to invest my energy in it.' Make 'I' statements and talk about yourself rather than about the other person; there's much more power in that. Getting into 'whys' is nearly always a mistake. Usually, the more times a person is asked, the more reasons they try to come up with. And that's not necessary. It's damaging to the self-esteem of both people."

In the world of romance, kissing frogs seems to come with the territory. Back in our single days, we kissed some ourselves—even jumped into the pond with a few. But you can keep your contact with cold, rubbery lips to a minimum by resolving to say no to unsuitable suitors and dead-end relationships. Next time you find yourself out on a date thinking, "Gee, I should really go home and do some laundry," let that be your cue. Throw that one back into the water.

And keep the faith. Remember, saying no is just a step along the way to a resounding, lifelong, satisfying *yes!*

# 5 Saying No to Family and Friends

*Your mother expects you to spend an hour or so on the phone listening to a detailed summary of her day. Every day.*

*Your cousin is calling to tell you what her adorable toddlers are wearing to your wedding. The only trouble is, the kids weren't invited.*

*As you're leaving for a vacation to Italy, a friend asks if you'd mind delivering a small gift to his relatives in Sorrento: a half gallon of authentic Vermont maple syrup.*

Where would we be without family and friends? We owe them so much—for their loyalty, their love, for making up our support system. And yet no matter how much we love some people, at times we want to clobber them for their insensitivity and thoughtlessness. At other times we just need a little distance from them.

This chapter looks at how to say no diplomatically to family and friends who overwhelm you, ask for too many favors, or make too many demands. We'll explore some of the most familiar scenarios that arise between parents and adult children, brothers and sisters, friends and neighbors, and we'll suggest techniques that can be applied in a wide range of situations.

In the long run, being able to say no to loved ones is a necessary skill for keeping these important relationships healthy and strong. By setting reasonable limits with demanding relatives and friends, you're taking steps to prevent animosity from festering and possibly exploding into an epic battle. Have you heard tales of family members who haven't spoken to each other for years but can't remember how the original feud got started? Chances are it was because someone didn't know how to say no.

Suppose your brother and his family stop by unannounced whenever they feel like taking a dip in your pool. When they do, you feel obliged to drop everything and play host. They eat all your food, use up all your clean towels, track wet footprints through your house, and never say thank you. To them it's fun; to you it's a big imposition. If you keep letting your resentment simmer under the surface, there's a fight waiting to happen.

Managing life's little tensions *as they arise* protects your heart from accumulated ill will and frees you up to enjoy your relationships more. It becomes easier to savor the warmth and caring that family and friends are all about. By fending off the bad stuff, you create more room for the good stuff.

We realize that for many people, the definitions of "family" and "friends" blur and overlap. Your sister might also be your best friend, or a few good friends may feel more like real family than your siblings do. In this chapter we've found it convenient to discuss certain situations in terms of either family or friends. But please consider them in whatever context has meaning for you.

## Life in the Inner Circle: The Usual Angst

Ideally, your inner circle of close friends and family is the place where you can most easily relax and be yourself. With the people you're closest to, you want to be able to say, "No, I'm too tired" or "No, it's not convenient for me to do that," without agonizing over the possible consequences.

However, the atmosphere inside the inner circle isn't always so amicable. At times the close nature of these relationships can make saying no more difficult.

There may be individuals—a parent, sibling, spouse, friend, or lover—who exert a power over you that others don't have. Perhaps they manipulate you by withholding affection or approval unless you do things their way. As a result, you may find yourself trying vainly to please, always saying yes in hopes of getting what you want and need from them. Others may intimidate you with their anger or belittle you by mocking your attempts to make your own decisions. Over time, they condition you to anticipate and dread their yelling or sarcastic comments. To spare yourself the trauma, you agree to whatever they ask and behave the way they want you to.

One forty-year-old woman we know explained that she still can't say no to her older brother, who has a lifelong pattern of ridiculing her tastes and interests. "I'm usually pretty assertive," she says. "But with him, I always seem to just give in and do things at his convenience. Whenever I try to stake a claim for myself, he has this ability to cut me down with some snide remark—like whatever I want to do is a stupid idea. And because he grew up doing that to me, he can make me believe it on some level."

Guilt is another powerful weapon that loved ones may use to control us. We say yes to their excessive demands out of fear that if we don't help, they will be very hurt or even come to harm.

While we expect to make sacrifices for the people we care about most, we may also need to protect ourselves from them. Loved ones have easy access to our most vulnerable spots, and they know how to take aim and hit us where it hurts. They can chip away at our self-esteem, drain our energy, disrupt our lives, and drive us crazy faster than anyone else.

In offering suggestions on how to set limits with the people you're closest to, we do not mean to oversimplify what might be a very complicated and troubled situation. Some people reading this book may be struggling to cope with parents or other family members who have hurt them badly. Some of you may have survived serious abuse or neglect, or perhaps you love someone who has. Destructive patterns can affect your ability to recognize and take care of your own needs.

If the very thought of saying no to a family member, friend, or lover provokes serious anxiety, you may need more support than we can offer in these pages. A good therapist can help you better understand and change harmful family patterns that may be continuing to this day.

We hope you will take steps to defend yourself against people who, for whatever reasons, control, degrade, or undermine you. Unlike children who must live with their parents for better or worse, as a determined adult you have the power to overcome difficult relationships.

In most cases a little preparation and some practical techniques can help you set limits and reclaim your space, time, and self-respect.

## Saying No to Put-Downs

Does a relative or friend make you wonder whether you have any backbone at all? Certain people are very difficult to say no to because you know exactly what will result: They're going to criticize your decision, put you down, or make sarcastic remarks at your expense. To avoid the verbal abuse, you cave in and let them have their way. Meanwhile, your self-esteem suffers.

If someone has a long-standing habit of pushing you around, it will be difficult to change his behavior. It's easier to change your own. Do that by announcing that this time the put-downs are not going to work. Letting him know that his words have no power over you is more effective than trying to argue any specific criticism he directs at you.

Standing up to someone who intimidates you requires a lot of determination. Frankly, this could be a "fake it till you make it" situation. You may not ever feel quite ready to make a statement like one of the following; perhaps you don't really believe in any of the statements yourself. But summon up your courage and say it anyway. Focus on your reason for saying no and envision the nasty comments bouncing off your skin, leaving you untouched. Recognize that these pathetic little weapons only work if you allow them to.

- *You really know how to push my buttons, but I'm learning how to do what's best for me.*
- *Calling me stupid isn't going to change my mind.*
- *You're very clever, but your sarcasm won't work this time.*
- *I'm really tired of your insults. I expect more support from a friend.*
- *I can see you're trying to hurt me with that comment. Nice try.*
- *I'm tuning you out. You've lost radio contact.*

## Saying No to Guilt-Tripping and Meddling

With some people, you feel especially guilty about saying no because that's exactly how they *want* you to feel. Plenty of parents, for example, are experts at inducing guilt in order to control their adult children's behavior. When their kids grow up, these parents can't quite let them run their own lives and make their own decisions.

It's one thing when you're eight years old and Mom scolds you for throwing a rock at the kid next door. Back then it was your parents' job to make you feel guilty for certain kinds of behavior. It was how they taught you right from wrong. And if they did their job well, you are now a solid citizen with a fully developed conscience. That means *you* now get to decide whether you've been good or bad.

With all due respect to your elders and the wisdom they imparted, you may have to set them straight about a few things. For example, that you're not a terrible person because you want to spend a holiday with your spouse's family once in a while. Or because you want to join a ballet company instead of the Marines. Isn't it fun being an adult and getting to decide these things for yourself?

## Guilt-Tripping for Attention

No matter how much time and attention you give some people, they want more.

Even when you feel fully justified in saying no, a talented guilt-tripper can still make you feel bad about it. There's no easy way to overcome that; guilt doesn't necessarily go away just because you tell it to. But if you are generous and attentive to this person a good deal of the time and know in your heart that you are, trust in the knowledge that with practice, the guilt will diminish. In the meantime, "fake it till you make it."

It's certainly not the worst thing in the world to have loved ones who crave your company. Express your gratitude often, but don't be afraid to take care of your own needs when you're feeling overwhelmed or exhausted. A few suggestions:

- *I love our visits, but I just can't come tonight. If I don't take care of some things at home, I'm going to get really stressed out. I don't want it to get to that point, so I'll see you next week instead.*
- *I've given you a lot of my time lately, but I have to say no this time. Please don't make me feel bad about it. That's not fair.*

Planning regularly scheduled visits (in person or on the phone) can be an effective strategy for coping with people who demand a lot of your time. Ideally, they will find the consistency reassuring, and you will find it easier to resist when they pressure you for attention at inopportune times.

- *You know how much I love seeing you, and I wish I could come more often, but I can't always do that. Why don't we count on having dinner together the first and third Wednesdays of every month? We'll make it a regular date.*
- *Dad, I wish I had time to talk on the phone every day. But my life is so hectic that it's just not possible. I'll call every Sunday and more if I can, but it wouldn't be fair to promise something I can't realistically do. So save up your good stories for our next conversation, because I want to hear them all.* (See also "On the Phone and Wanting Off," page 182.)

Say no by reminding the guilt-tripper that other people need you, too.

- *Mom, I'm sure you understand why we need to spend some holidays with Ted's family, too. They want to see us as much as you do. Please be generous about this.*
- *We hate to miss Christmas at your house, Aunt Lydia, but this year we've decided to take the family skiing for the holidays. It's something we promised the kids, and it's the only chance we'll have this winter. I know you'll understand. Will you freeze some leftovers for us?*

### Standing Up to Meddlers

Parents, grandparents, stepparents, siblings, aunts, uncles, and others may feel they have the right to tell you how to run your life. You have the right to tell them politely to mind their own business. The following suggestions may help put an end to unwelcome advice from well-intentioned loved ones.

- *I know we'll never see eye to eye on this, but let's agree to disagree.*
- *I appreciate that you want what's best for me, but I'd appreciate it more if you'd trust me to make my own decisions and learn my own lessons.*
- *I'm sorry you don't like my apartment/house/neighborhood,*

*but I'm very happy here. I have no intention of moving, so
please don't bring it up again.*

- *I know you don't like Phil, but my romantic life is one area
  where I'm not looking for a second opinion. Thanks for caring, but I need to make my own choices.*
- *I know I'd make more money if I followed in your foot-
  steps, but it's important to me to express myself as an
  artist/dancer/musician. Even if it means I live more simply
  than you want me to, I hope you can be happy that I'm
  doing something that I find so satisfying.*
- *Whether or not to have a child is one of the most personal
  decisions I'll ever make. I hope you'll respect my privacy
  and stop asking. If and when I have a baby, it will be my
  decision.*
- *Sis, I know you don't approve of the way I'm raising my
  children, but I'm doing what I think is best, and I'd appreciate your support rather than your criticism.*

### Enough Is Enough

If the meddling and guilt-mongering continue despite your best
efforts, try ending the conversation the way Mom and Dad did
once upon a time.

- *Mom, you taught me once that "no is a complete sentence."
  So there's nothing more to talk about.*
- *Dad, remember what you always used to say: "My house,
  my rules." Well, we're in my house, now . . . and I'm making the rules!*
- *I say this to the kids all the time, and now I have to say it
  to you: No means no. Let's drop it, okay?*
- *When I was little, you said when I grew up I'd be free to do
  whatever I want. Well, I'm grown up now. And I want to
  live in Hoboken—I'm not moving back to Poughkeepsie!*

## The Importance of Being Honest

Here's why we believe a firm, clear "no" is better than a wishy-washy "yes."

Have you ever made a date with a friend who, when the day arrived:

— called with a last-minute excuse, leaving you high and dry?

— showed up late and/or announced she'd have to leave early?

— showed up completely unprepared, e.g., without money or an essential item?

— spent the whole time looking at her watch, or complaining about the food, the service, or the noise in the restaurant?

— "forgot" about your date and didn't show up at all?

You probably wished your friend had said no in the first place and saved you the aggravation.

People who habitually agree to do things they don't want to do may think they're being "nice." But cooperative as they seem, they often give their true feelings away in other, less direct ways, like those listed above. Intentionally or not, they "punish" you by creating some obstacle or signaling nonverbally that they'd rather be somewhere else. Technically, they're doing what you asked, but they manage to let you know they're not pleased.

We all know how infuriating it is to be on the receiving end of this kind of passive-aggressive behavior. But at times, we probably all act this way. Learning to say no more easily will help you avoid behaving like this yourself because you'll spend less time engaged in things you resent doing.

And if you want to cut down on exasperating incidents with friends and loved ones, think about what happens when they say no to *you*.

## Say No . . . But Listen for It, Too

The act of saying no is a two-character drama in which we play the part of either speaker or listener. Both roles are equally significant. In the speaker's role, we can say no clearly and directly or cloud our meaning with ambiguous or deceptive language. As the listener, if we hear the "no" at all, we can choose to accept it or not.

If the person saying no to us is a spouse or partner, good friend or relative, we're apt to try changing his mind, using pressure tactics like pleading, cajoling, threatening, bargaining, or guilt-tripping. It's almost as if the closer the relationship, the harder it is for us to take no for an answer.

There's nothing wrong with using a little persuasion on friends or family. Sometimes people just need a push. But at a certain point, pushing becomes counterproductive. If you put others through the wringer because they've said no to you, it may discourage them from saying it in the future. But a "yes" induced under pressure may be more trouble than it's worth.

On the other hand, when loved ones feel free to be honest and say no to you, there's no need for passive-aggressive behavior. When you allow them to save more of their "yeses" for things *they* really care about, you'll eliminate many sources of tension between you. And you'll feel more comfortable saying no when it's your turn.

We tend to expect a lot from the people we love, and that's as it should be. But at times the wisest thing we can do is to relax our requirements a little. You might be surprised at how good it can feel to let go of some of your demands. Friends of ours recently told us a story that drove this point home.

Virginia and her husband Tom were invited away for the weekend by a business friend of Virginia's who had a house in the country. She looked forward to it for a month, but as the weekend approached, Tom became more and more vocal about not wanting to go. He wouldn't know anyone there, he said, and besides, he had work to do. Virginia, very disappointed and a little angry, lobbied hard to change Tom's mind—she pleaded, cajoled, etc. But all her entreaties just increased the tension between them. The more she pushed, the more he resisted, and the worse they both felt.

Eventually Virginia realized something that was both obvious and startling: Tom had a right to say no. His feelings were not unreasonable. At the same time, she didn't have to depend on him to enjoy her much-anticipated weekend. She could go without him! It wasn't exactly how she'd planned it, but it was a better option than staying home and seething. Once she recognized this, she stopped pressuring her husband. She told him—sincerely, not resentfully—that she didn't mind if he stayed home. Immediately she felt freer and happier.

But a funny thing happened. When Tom saw that Virginia was prepared to go without him, he decided he wanted to go, too. So he did—and he had a great time.

Sometimes, when you're willing to walk away from something, it falls right into your hands. By abandoning her struggle to change Tom's mind—by accepting his "no"—Virginia worked relationship magic. She released him from the stress of an unwelcome demand and liberated herself from having to depend on *his* decision in order to enjoy *her* weekend. And in the process, she got exactly what she wanted!

We can't promise that by learning to accept "no" as gracefully as you say it, you will always be as lucky as Virginia. But in the long run, you *will* be rewarded. Your generosity to the people you're close to will encourage them to be generous to you. By demonstrating that you respect their right to set reasonable limits with you—to say no occasionally—you set exactly the right example and invite them to give you the same consideration.

## Attached at the Hip?

Some people might consider it odd that Virginia was prepared to spend a weekend away from her husband. But is there a law that says couples must do everything together? When it's *you* who wants to say no, you may first have to abandon the idea that the two of you are attached at the hip. Another friend, Maria, did just that and solved a big problem in the process.

In the first few years she and Jeff were married, Maria always went along with him to visit his parents. She took it for granted that as Jeff's wife, her attendance was not only expected but required. But whenever they got together, Maria and her mother-in-law locked horns over one thing or another. "It takes a lot of energy and patience to put up with her," says Maria. "She meddles constantly. It's hard to take under the best of circumstances. But when I'm not feeling my best, I have no tolerance for it."

Maria resented spending her valuable free time with someone who harped on her constantly. She let Jeff know how she felt about his mother. "He felt trapped in the middle. Obviously, he wanted us both to get along. But we don't. That's the reality."

Eventually Maria realized a way to improve the situation: She began to say no and opt out of some of these visits. "I would call my mother-in-law and tell her, 'I'm not up to it.' She tends to pry, and would ask, 'Well, why not?' and I would keep repeating, 'I'm just not up to it.' She doesn't really consider that a legitimate reason. She'd prefer me to say either that I was sick or had to work. But I didn't want to have to make excuses all the time. In the beginning, it caused a lot of trouble. Saying no in such a straightforward way just isn't done in their family. But over time, she's come to accept it. She still pries to some degree, but not as much. It's better all around. I'm not forced into going, and everyone's happier. Through the process she's come to understand that there have got to be some boundaries."

As Maria sees it, the greatest benefit of saying no in this situation was that it relieved a great deal of stress in her marriage. "The situation with Jeff's mother had been causing tremendous difficulty between us. We fought about it all the time. Because he always felt pressure to have me go, he would put pressure on me. He worried that my saying no hurt his mother's feelings.

"Over time, I got him to understand that this wasn't about him. He doesn't have to take responsibility for my relationship with his mother, and he doesn't have to defend me. Since he's gotten that point, it's been much better. Now sometimes he'll take our daughter and go visit his folks without me. They have a nice, friendly visit, and I get some time to myself. The key was getting him to understand that I'm entitled to say no sometimes, and it's better for everyone if I do."

Maria feels that setting limits on time spent with her in-laws has improved her attitude about the time they do spend together.

"If I had continued to go along, feeling manipulated into doing these things, it would only have gotten worse. But now I have a different perspective on the whole thing. I know I can get some space when I need it, and that frees me from a lot of frustration and bitterness. Things aren't perfect, but they're better than they ever were."

By telling her mother-in-law, "I'm not up to it," without further explanation, Maria certainly rocked the family boat. But she said no the way she knew best, and for a good cause: to take care of her own needs and preserve a happy relationship with her husband. Eventually the waves subsided as her in-laws came to terms with Maria's occasional absences.

You may feel more comfortable using Face-Saving Excuses to get out of a recurring unpleasant situation. Sometimes that's the kindest method as well as the most practical and efficient. But think about whether your relationship is such that by being sincere, you can move it forward to a better, more open place. While you may face some opposition at first, you could, like Maria, set a process in motion that leads the other person to back off and impose on you less.

### Saying No to Full-Time Togetherness

When your partner pressures you to go somewhere you don't want to go or do something you don't want to do, and you end up going anyway, there's a good chance neither of you will have a good time. It works both ways: There may be times you'll have more fun on your own without having to worry about whether your mate is having a good time.

This is not to say that couples shouldn't make sacrifices for each other or compromise when they can. Still, on some occasions a response like one of the following can free you from the trap of full-time togetherness. (See also the suggestions for "Let's Socialize on My Terms—for a Change," page 134.)

- *Honey, I really appreciate that you're picking out the new TV for the living room. And you know how bored I get in electronics stores. I trust you to make a good choice, and I especially appreciate your not making me come with you.*
- *You have such a good time when you get together with your college roommates. And I know you'll want to reminisce a lot. I'd just feel like an outsider in that group, so why don't you go ahead to the reunion without me, and have a great time.*
- *I'm sure you'll have a terrific time at the game with the boys, but I really don't feel like going. I need a day to myself.*
- *I'm sure your office holiday party is a lot of fun, but it's a lot more fun for those of you who work together. I'll bow out this year and baby-sit. Go ahead and enjoy yourself. Just don't stand under the mistletoe.*

### "Stay Home, Honey"

There may be times when you're the one who's going, and you'd prefer not to have your partner tag along. A preemptive "no" is useful in these situations.

- *I know you hate to spend a weekend apart, and I'll miss you, too. But it's so rare that I have a chance to get together with my sisters. You'd be bored to tears anyway with all the "girl talk." Thanks for being so understanding, sweetheart.*

## Family Functions

"It's totally out of control," Melissa says, sighing. "I come from a big family, and somebody's always celebrating something. I can't tell you how many weekends I've had to plan around these family events: bridal showers, baby showers, christenings, birthday parties, First Communions. . . . I love my family, but enough already."

Some people would give anything to be part of a large, close-knit clan like Melissa's. Others will readily understand her complaint. It *is* possible to have too much family togetherness, especially if you're trying to manage a busy, active life of your own.

Of course, if you simply stop showing up for family events, eventually they'll stop inviting you. But there are less drastic ways of creating some much-needed space from your family.

### Saying No to Family Overexposure

What sets family events apart from most other social events is that they generally involve the same recurring cast of characters. This is good and bad.

On one hand, you can opt out of the less important gatherings knowing you'll soon see everyone at a more significant event. On the other hand, not everyone agrees on what a significant event is. Many family members we've known and loved are highly competitive with each other. They love to keep score (as in "You saw Aunt Julia twice last month. Why can't you come here?").

With loved ones like these, fairness—or at least, the appearance of fairness—is something to strive for. This is where developing a Policy can be extremely helpful. It's simply a matter of deciding in advance what sort of family occasions you're going to say yes to. Depending on the size of your family and the number of invitations they extend, you'll know best where to draw the line.

### A Family Policy "With Justice for All"

Here are some suggestions to help you start forming your Policy guidelines for family events:

- Marriages: Make the wedding itself your priority. Then decide whether you want to include any related festivities in your Policy, such as showers and engagement parties. For example, you might say yes to the wedding and one other event, but no more than that.
- Bridal showers: See above. You could also decide to attend for first marriages only or for relatives up to the rank of first cousin.
- Baby showers: Attend if it's her first child but not if it's her second, third, or tenth. The baby won't know the difference; besides, you'll send a *lovely* gift.
- Religious rites of passage (e.g., christening, bris, First Communion, confirmation, bar/bat mitzvah): To avoid arousing jealousy, be aware of the need for a consistent Policy toward relatives of the same rank: If you're there for your brother's daughter, it's wise to be there for your sister's son, too.
- Graduations: Attend when someone finishes high school or college.
- Religious or traditional holidays: Often the issue is where to celebrate. You can make it a Policy to visit your parents and in-laws in alternate years or start a new tradition and invite the whole tribe to your house.

Next time you're invited to a "non-Policy" event, you could say:

- *You know, I love getting together with the family, but lately I've been feeling the need to cut back on all the parties and events I go to. So I've developed a policy I hope will be fair to everyone. From now on, I'm only going to graduation parties when someone finishes high school or college. So I'll have to pass this time. But please give Zoe a big kiss for me and congratulate her on finishing second grade.* (Optional: *Does she have a copy of* Green Eggs and Ham? *I'd like to send her one to mark the occasion.)*

## Weddings: Let Them Eat Cake (Without You)

Don't underestimate the importance of weddings—if not to you, then to the key people involved. Where you have a close connection, others will remember if you don't show up for their big event and may hold a grudge forever. If you're going to feel guilty about not going, that probably means you should go. On the other hand, if you're surprised to be invited at all, it's probably okay to skip it.

Luckily, most weddings are easy to say no to: You simply check the line on the RSVP card that says "I will not attend." (Including a handwritten note is a nice gesture. Wish the couple well, and tell them you'll be there in spirit.)

Occasionally, however, you may find yourself in the unusual position of having to defend your decision to someone other than the person who invited you. This could happen if, for example, your mother calls to give you a hard time about not attending your second cousin's wedding. She may be acutely conscious of how her own cousin—the bride's mother—will view your absence. Even if the bride herself doesn't care a whit whether you attend, others may have their own reasons for wanting you there.

### Saying No to Third-Party Pressure

When someone other than the bride or groom is pressuring you, fend them off without guilt.

- *Mom, I just don't have the time or the energy to go to this wedding. My job keeps me running all week, and I really*

*need my weekends to take care of everything else in my
life. Besides, I barely know the bride. I'd like to get to
know her better, but weddings aren't a good place for that
anyway. (Optional: Why don't we plan on a family dinner
with the newlyweds in a month or two when things settle
down?)*

- *I love you and I love to see you, but I can't stand these
noisy weddings where the band is so loud that you can't
even talk. I'll come over next Sunday, and we'll spend the
afternoon together.*

- *I really want to spend time with you and Grandpa, but I
don't want to share you with two hundred other people.
Let's make plans to get together, just us.*

And if you could never get away with the above:
- *I won't be able to come—I have long-standing plans that
can't be changed.* Most mothers we know will then ask,
"What plans?" At which point you can tell her to stop
being so nosy, or resort to Face-Saving Excuses. Here are a
few suggestions:
- *We have tickets to the theater that night.*
- *We have reservations at the shore for that weekend.*
- *We have a business function that night.*
- *I've already accepted an invitation to another wedding—a
friend from work is getting married on the same day.*

## Always a Bridesmaid? Saying No Gracefully

For the bride, it's the experience of a lifetime. But for you it's
the fourth trip down the aisle this year. While it's certainly a
blessing to have so many close friends, being asked to join too
many wedding parties within a relatively short period can seriously drain your time and energy, not to mention your bank
account. The shopping . . . the fittings . . . the lavender shoes.
Before you reluctantly sign on for another hitch, consider
whether you'd be happier sitting on the sidelines this time.

**"I Do...Not"**

If after careful consideration your answer is no, you could say any of the following:

- *It makes me feel so good that you asked me, and normally I'd say yes in a minute. But I've been a bridesmaid several times recently, and my resources are exhausted. I know you'll understand if I don't join the wedding party.*
- *I'm so flattered that you asked me. Still, I can't afford the expense of the dress, the engagement gift, the wedding gift, and the time required for all the pre-wedding festivities if I'm in the wedding party. I'd much rather save my resources and give you a meaningful wedding gift. I wouldn't miss your wedding for the world, but I'm afraid I'll have to turn down the honor of being a bridesmaid.*
- *Thank you so much for asking, but I have to say no. I recently turned down a similar request from my sister-in-law, and I'm afraid that whole side of the family would be terribly offended if I were to be in your wedding.*

## Is This a "Yes" in Disguise?

You're not close to the bride, though she's a relative, and you never met the groom. It's an evening wedding a hundred miles away, so unless you get a hotel room, you'll have to face a long drive home in the dark (and forgo the cocktails). Since the kids aren't invited, you'll need to make arrangements for them, too. You'll have to shop for something decent to wear. On the face of it, the whole thing is a big pain in the neck.

But before you say no, try looking at the situation from another angle. Will your beloved grandmother be there, whom you don't see nearly enough? Will attending the wedding give you a rare chance to reminisce with all your cousins in one place? Have you been thinking that you'd like to be closer to your family in the future? Would a night in a hotel, away from the kids, be a nice break for you and your husband?

This book is about learning to say no in order to make

time for what's really meaningful in life. In order to do that, we must know how to recognize a meaningful experience when we see it.

What at first seems like a bothersome obligation can turn out to be something else entirely. A family event may offer many benefits to enjoy and savor—if you know where to look. Don't send your regrets until you've thought about whether, despite the inconveniences, this event might be a "yes" in disguise: precisely the type of occasion that you're saying no to other things in order to do. How often do you get the opportunity to celebrate something happy, see people who love you, and nurture your ties to family and friends?

For some people, commemorating special events with family represents the most joyous time in their lives, providing memories that stay with them forever. Even if you don't mind missing the event, your presence might mean a great deal to someone else, such as an elderly relative. Being able to make someone very happy can be satisfying enough in itself.

At the very least, showing up at a large gathering gives you plenty of "face time" with the family, which could make it easier if you have to say no the next time.

And if you're single, you might hit it off with a friend of the groom.

Maybe it's worth the extra trouble of getting there.

## Funerals

Invitations are seldom issued for funerals. But in some families, not showing up for a funeral can spark a decades-long feud. Therefore, we are not going to offer advice on how to get out of going. If you *are* asked to be at a funeral, it's probably because your presence would bring comfort to someone who is suffering a loss. Perhaps you don't even remember your great-aunt Emma, who raised your mother. But if she was important to Mom, and Mom's important to you, be there for her.

## Saying No to Holiday Overkill

Around holiday time, virtually everyone we know complains about three things:
1. Rampant commercialism
2. Being too busy
3. Spending too much money

Nothing saps the holiday spirit like having to run around and buy gifts you don't have time to shop for, can't afford, and that nobody really needs anyway. If you're part of an extended family that engages in a great deal of gift-giving, that scenario may sound familiar.

Perhaps you're fed up with the whole process. You could simply refuse to participate in your family's long-standing traditions—if you don't mind looking like the Grinch Who Said No to Christmas. Or you could propose a new family tradition: one that says yes to family togetherness, generosity, and fun. (The fact that it also cuts down on aggravation and saves you time and money is a nice benefit.)

Suggest one or more of the following to relatives or friends with whom you normally exchange gifts. Test it on your immediate family the first time, and if it's a success, share it with siblings, in-laws, and other relatives.

- A grab bag or Secret Santa program is ideal for families who are ready to cut down on multiple-present-buying. Set a maximum spending limit. Pick a name out of a bowl, buy that person a gift. It's simple, economical, and fun!
- Instead of individual gifts, buy a gift for the entire household, e.g., a video collection, Ping-Pong table, or board games.
- Designate an "official" gift for everyone to exchange. For instance, make it an all-books holiday, or all pajamas, or all garden supplies. It's fun to see how everyone interprets the assignment—and it sure simplifies the decision-making process.
- Plan a "trading only" holiday. Instead of shopping for new

things, everyone must present something he or she already owns to another person who would like it.

- Instead of gifts, exchange coupons offering to perform a service for the recipient. Family members can tap their own interests and skills: promise a manicure/pedicure, garden work, home or auto repair, a good meal, sewing or clothing repair, chauffeur service—you name it!
- Pool your money and invest in a photographic family portrait with prints for everyone.
- Give gift certificates to your loved ones' favorite stores. Designate a maximum amount. In most cases, you can order them by phone or on-line.
- Invest in experiences instead of material things. For example, plan an outing or vacation as a family to someplace everyone would enjoy. You might rent a house in a ski area or visit a national park. Or go to a show together. It doesn't have to be a Broadway extravaganza to become a memorable family tradition.
- Make a donation in honor of your family: Plant a tree, "adopt" a needy child, contribute to a cause or organization you all support. It's a great way to celebrate the true spirit of giving.

For the new tradition to take hold, other family members have to get behind the idea, too. Your job is to convince them that what you're proposing will relieve much of the pressure of the season, while enhancing the family's experience of the holidays. They may not need much convincing. Since women usually take on the lion's share of responsibility for the holidays, get in touch with the other "matriarchs" in your family to test your proposal and see if you get an enthusiastic response.

By all means, don't try to discourage people from holiday-related activities they truly enjoy, like baking, tree-trimming, or decorating the house. Keep in mind that your goal as a family is to say no to those aspects of the season that just add to the burden for everyone. Save more of your resources and invest them in celebrating and being together.

## "Eat, Eat!": Saying No to Aggressive Feeders

Some family members don't understand how the words "no" and "food" can ever be used in the same sentence. It's not so much that they love to eat. What they really love is to see *you* eat. This means that if you're on a special diet, you've eaten enough, or you're simply not hungry, special skills are needed to keep these people from pushing food on you.

The best approach to refusing food is to pay enthusiastic homage to the person who cooked it. This is one area where context is everything: It's not how much you eat, but how much you marvel at every morsel. Heap lots of praise on the server. Give her all the credit she's looking for. Even if you eat like a bird, exclaim loudly how delicious everything is. Fuss over the table and about how beautiful everything looks. Don't worry about overdoing it—you can't.

### Phase I: Setting the Stage

- *Gloria, you made lasagna! I've waited all year for this!*
- *Sis, I started thinking about your Thanksgiving dinner around Labor Day, and I've been thinking about it ever since!*
- (Sniff, sniff) *Is that Helen's onion soup I smell? Oh, boy, we're in for a treat!*

### Phase II: Dinner-Table Tactics

Take small portions at first, so you can make a big show of asking for seconds.

- *Omigod, Grandma! These potato pancakes are incredible! I've got to have more!*

### Phase III: Saying No

- *It sure looks delicious. I wish I had room for it.*
- *I really can't eat another bite.*
- *My taste buds are screaming yes, but my stomach is screaming no.*
- *I'll explode if I eat another bite. But I definitely want to take some home. Will you make me up a doggy bag before I go?*
- *Mom, I know you want me to have more, but I'm full. Since food is your way of expressing love, why don't you give me a hug instead?*

### Special Diets

Dieters, vegetarians, and others on restricted diets for medical or religious reasons often find themselves in situations where they must turn down food that's being offered. When invited out, you can cope by snacking before you leave home or bringing along a dish you can eat. But that doesn't solve the problem of how to say "no thanks" to Grandma's roast beef without hurting her feelings. If you fear that the cook will be disappointed you're not joining in, it's appropriate to tip her off in advance to your new eating habits. Be gracious; don't expect her to cater to you, though she'll probably want to.

- *I've made a commitment to a new diet, so I won't be eating as much as I usually do over the holidays. I wanted to let you know in advance so you won't be surprised.*
- *I'm really looking forward to dinner at your house! I wanted to let you know that I've become a vegetarian. I hope that won't be a problem.* (If the chef asks for suggestions, pasta is always a good choice.)

Offering to bring a dish is a gracious way of getting around the problem—and assuring you'll have something you like to eat.

- *Can I bring a salad/side dish/dessert?*

If you run up against resistance about your diet, citing a doctor's advice can add credibility to your argument.

- *My doctor told me I should avoid cholesterol for the next few months.*

When you must say no in advance to a particular dish, appeal to the cook's pride by asking her to make something special for you.

- *Since I won't be eating the ham at Easter dinner, do you think you could make your famous grilled eggplant on the side? I'm crazy about it!*

Many cooks love the opportunity to talk about how they prepared a dish and what ingredients they used. To divert attention from the foods you're saying no to, focus on those you *are* eating.

- *Really, Grandma, I've stopped eating meat, and I'm very serious about it. But I absolutely love these string beans. I think the sign of a truly good cook is the ability to cook vegetables well. Did you marinate these first?*
- *Now that I'm on a no-meat, no-dairy diet, can you give me some of your favorite recipes for vegetable dishes?*

## I Love You, But . . .

The flip side of being the good, kind person you are is that you're also fair game for relatives and friends who would take advantage of your pleasant nature. Now we'll look at how you can retain your pleasant nature and have a pleasant time, too, by saying no to impositions and other common conflicts that arise between loved ones.

## No Houseguests

Keeping houseguests away is a lot easier than getting rid of them. Once they're under your roof, it's almost impossible to evict someone in a graceful, guilt-free manner. Which is why, if you want to limit guests' stays or keep them at bay altogether, prevention is the technique of choice.

Use these responses when prospective houseguests are headed your way:

### Keeping Them Away

- *You're coming to town? Fantastic! A great new hotel/bed and breakfast just opened—you'll love it!*
- *I'd love to see you, but I'm afraid I can't invite you to stay over. It's not a good time for us to have houseguests.*
- *I can't wait to see you! Do you need recommendations on a good place to stay?*

### Limiting the Stay

Do this by specifying which days you'd like them to visit.

- *I'm so glad you're planning to come to town! Can you stay over Friday and Saturday nights?*
- *It will be great to see you—why don't you stay over here one night?*
- *Why don't you plan on spending your last night in town here with us?*

### When You Have to Say No

- *Sorry, the timing is bad.*
- *We'd love to put you up, but we simply don't have the space.*
- *The house is in no condition for guests right now.*
- *The kids have so many friends coming and going. It's like Grand Central Station around here. Can I help you find a good hotel?*

- *I wish we could have you, but you wouldn't be comfortable here.*
- *We turned our guest room into a home office . . . and with everybody using it and the computer on half the night, it's the busiest room in the house! I'm afraid we just don't have the space for overnight guests.*

## Sorry, No Kids Allowed

Some parents, when receiving an invitation, automatically assume it extends to their children as well. This can complicate things, especially if you're planning a dinner party and looking forward to a little grown-up conversation with friends.

To prevent surprise appearances by other people's children, make your "adults only" preference clear *before* the day of the event. The most gracious way to do so is to extend an invitation specifying only the names of those who *are* welcome. To issue a verbal invitation, say something like:

- *We're having some people over for dinner on the twenty-first. I hope you and Jack will be able to come.*

If that seems too subtle, communicate your "no kids" message this way:

- *We thought it would be fun to plan a "grown-ups' night" for a change. (Or: This will give all you parents a night out without the kids for a change.)*

When asked outright whether kids are welcome at a particular gathering, answer:

- *Not this time, I'm afraid. This party wouldn't be appropriate for kids. I hope you can get a baby-sitter and join us.*

And what about that relative who assumed her kids were invited to your wedding even though they clearly weren't?

- *Sorry, I'm afraid you misunderstood. We're not having any children at the wedding.*

Anyone who is thoughtless enough to arrive with kids in tow despite your obvious wishes deserves to be crossed off the guest list permanently.

## Ask My Permission First

It's hard to say no when you haven't been asked in the first place. Family and friends may impose on you without asking permission, and assume everything's fine. To prevent a repeat performance, say no preemptively with a statement like one of the following.

- *You know I love seeing you and the kids, but I need to know in advance if you want to visit. Please call first from now on.*
- *Everyone has been coming here for Thanksgiving for years, but I need a break. Either someone else can do it this year, or we'll all go out to a restaurant.*
- *Claire, when you ask to borrow my jewelry or clothes, you know I'm usually happy to say yes. But I get upset when you take things without asking. If I'm not here, please wear something of your own.* (See also " 'Don't Touch My Stuff!': How Not to Be a Lender," page 144.)

## Stifle the Racist, Sexist Comments

Have you ever wondered how you could possibly be related to such narrow-minded people? At times loved ones may act in very unlovable ways.

There you are enjoying a holiday dinner with the family, and Uncle Hank makes an offensive racist remark. Or Cousin Mel tells a sexist joke that's thoroughly unfunny. Or Aunt Ruth starts expounding on society's woes and which ethnic group is to blame for them all.

Do you sit quietly and say nothing, implying that you agree and find it all perfectly acceptable? Or do you speak up for the values of justice, equality, and respect for all human beings? You don't want to shirk your moral obligation to denounce these Neanderthal attitudes—but on the other hand, you know how Uncle Hank gets. Give him a little fuel and he'll go on all night. Perhaps what you really want is to register your protest *and* shut the bigot up.

By all means, if you're up for a good fight, don't let us deter you. It's just that in our experience, it's virtually impossible to "enlighten" someone during a dinner-table debate; instead, people tend to dig in their heels and become more adamant (and louder). But while it may be unrealistic to think you can change an offensive relative's point of view, you do have the right to insist on a certain standard of behavior in your presence. Voicing your disapproval may cause him to think twice before speaking that way again, at least while you're around. It lets him know that his insulting remarks will not go unchallenged and makes him a little less comfortable. And it affirms the principles you believe in—to him and to everyone else in the vicinity.

Challenging someone's views is confrontational by definition. There's no guarantee that you can do so without provoking a negative reaction. To avoid being pulled into a long, heated argument, keep the focus on expressing your objection to the remark and letting the person know it offends you. These phrases, with variations, can serve as your first and last words on the matter. Repeat them as often as necessary.

**Saying No to Racists or Sexist Comments and Ethnic Slurs**
- *Please don't talk that way around me.*
- *That's not a fact; that's your opinion. And it's one I strongly disagree with.*
- *I have to object to that remark. Every human being is entitled to respect. Your attitude offends me.*
- *Please don't tell jokes like that in my presence. I don't find them funny at all.*
- *I know you're an intelligent person, so I'm suprised you'd make a remark like that.*

- *Everyone has character flaws. The person you're talking about may have character flaws. But his nationality has nothing to do with it. We don't need to perpetuate that kind of prejudice.*
- *It's hard to believe anyone still thinks that way in this day and age. I thought we were beyond those old stereotypes.*
- *I think this conversation is getting ugly. Let's change the subject.*

In your home and around your children, assert your authority.

- *The Policy: In this house we don't tolerate talk like that. My children know better than to put down people of other nationalities/races. Maybe you could learn something from them about treating people fairly.*
- *I wouldn't be doing my job as a parent if I let that remark pass without saying anything. That is exactly the opposite of what we're teaching our kids. We don't share your biased views, and we don't appreciate your spreading them around here.*
- *You can believe whatever you want to believe, but I don't want you talking that way in my house.*

Sometimes people who disparage other races or ethnic groups are themselves members of a group that's suffered from discrimination and stereotyping. If that's the case, remind them of this.

- *How do you feel when someone says* (our people) *are all _____? You don't think it's fair when people use negative stereotypes to judge our entire group. Why is it fair when you do it?*
- *Hasn't* (our group) *had to put up with discrimination? Haven't we learned anything from it?*

To end the discussion, you may have to tell the offensive person:

- *I don't see the point of getting into a fight with you. We don't see eye to eye, and that's that.*

## Don't Treat Me Like Family, Treat Me Better

Between friends, conflicts can arise because each party brings different expectations to the relationship, and each party is influenced by her own family's culture.

Pamela told us about an incident with Belinda, an inner-circle friend and co-worker from, as Pamela describes it, "a huge, dysfunctional family."

"She was getting married, and I made her a wedding shower at my parents' house. I planned the whole thing, spent time, energy, and money, and I was pleased to do it. I *wanted* to do it. And it came off beautifully.

"It so happened that the following weekend her sister was giving a shower for family members and close friends only. (The one I gave was primarily for work people.) But I was in graduate school at the time, with finals coming up, and under the circumstances, I didn't think I needed to attend two showers on two successive weekends. So I called to say I couldn't come. Belinda blew up at me. Because in her family you couldn't get away with things like that."

It's ironic that their differences arose because Belinda considered Pamela "part of the family." As such, she expected Pamela to behave the way she and her relatives did, which can be summed up as "Be there for me, no matter what." What Belinda regarded as loyalty, Pamela regarded as excessively demanding.

Friends can be just as demanding—and unreasonable—as family members. Even when your friends are very important to you, the price of membership in their inner circle may sometimes be high.

## Let's Socialize on My Terms—for a Change

Friends with forceful personalities may often coerce you into doing things you don't really want to do. If you're always adapting to someone else's wishes, you may feel the need to restore some balance. Think about whether part of the problem may be due to a lack of focus on your part. When you have a clear sense of how you like (and don't like) to spend your time, it becomes easier to assert yourself.

### Finding Harmony

When planning dates with others, all parties must expect to compromise a bit. Don't be afraid of disagreements—they're perfectly normal between friends. The goal here is to find an activity you can all be happy with. To say no to a friend's suggestion, try one of these strategies:

Option 1: Propose something else.
- *Sorry, Rich. I really don't feel like seeing* Die Hard XII *tonight. How about* A Man and a Woman *at the revival house? . . . Okay, why don't we just skip the movie and go have a nice dinner instead?*
- *I'm not in the mood for Norwegian food tonight. Why don't we try that new Icelandic restaurant? . . . No? Then suggest something else.*

Option 2: Split up and meet later.
- *I think I'll pass on the Monster Truck rally. I just wouldn't be able to appreciate it. But I can tell you really want to go, so why don't we plan on meeting up afterward?*
- *Why don't you call me when your backgammon game is over, and I'll meet you afterward? There's plenty I could be doing in the meantime.*

Option 3: If you truly can't agree, respect your priorities and make a new date if necessary.

- *I've been waiting since the seventies to see Engelbert Humperdinck, and he's only going to be in town one night. I'm dying to see him, so if you don't want to come, I'll need to reschedule our date. What are you doing next Saturday?*

### Buying Tickets

Making dates for the theater, concerts, or sports events with friends leads to the question of who will pick up the tickets. Some friends are always "too busy." Next time preempt them with:

- *I'd love to go to the concert, if you can pick up the tickets. I have a hectic week ahead, and I won't be able to get to the box office.*

If your friend still makes excuses, say:
- *Then why don't you call Ticketmaster and order them over the phone?*

The service charge is worth paying if it prevents you from feeling manipulated by your friend.

### When Playing Host

Feel free to use the "split up and meet later" approach when out-of-town guests want to visit a sight you've seen quite often enough.

- *You'll have a great time at the dental-floss factory—it's something everyone should see once in their lives. Since I've already seen it, let's plan on meeting for lunch after you're done, okay?*

## No Sale

There's nothing like being cornered by a zealous friend who has something to sell. The word "squirm" was invented for such occasions.

Having a personal relationship with the seller does not obligate you to purchase a water filter, vacuum cleaner, colorful algae, or any other product. Friendship, however, does make saying no more difficult.

If you've got your reasons, that should be reason enough. Either you don't need it, don't use it, don't want to pay for it, or don't want to get involved. Any additional pressure applied by a friend or relative is pure exploitation and guilt-tripping. Is that any way to run a business?

Next time you find yourself on the receiving end of a friend's sales pitch, these techniques can help you slip away gracefully.

- Try to stop the conversation as early as possible. It saves time for both of you—and it's a lot easier to resist a pitch you haven't actually heard.
- Be supportive of her efforts and wish her success.
- Respond with a simple explanation for your no. Be firm, stick to your answer, and repeat yourself as often as necessary.

The following responses can be adapted for any number of products likely to be sold by your friends, relatives, and co-workers.

### General
- *I'm afraid this water filter just isn't in my budget.*
- *Sorry, I'm not in the market—I never use those products.*
- *I just don't have a need for it.*
- *That's a very impressive vacuum cleaner. If I were in the market for something so powerful, I would definitely consider it. But the one I have works fine, and I'm happy with it. Thanks anyway.*

### Health-Related
- *What you're saying about the health benefits of co-enzyme Q-10 sounds interesting. And maybe it's all perfectly true. But I don't believe in taking things I don't feel any need for.*

- *I'm very committed to staying healthy through diet and exercise. Food supplements aren't part of the program for me. But thanks anyway.*

### Cleaning Products
- *Frankly, the products I use now do the job very well, and they're a lot less expensive. It wouldn't make sense for me to switch. So I have to say no, thanks.*
- *I buy my cleaning supplies in bulk at Price Club, and I currently have enough to last me for the next three years. Come back and ask me then.*
- *My housekeeper insists I buy the other brand. She'll have a fit if I buy something different.*

### Girl Scout Cookies, Candy Bars, Etc.
- *I'm a vegetarian. There are animal products in these cookies, so I don't want to buy any.*
- *I've made a commitment to avoid sugar, so I've gotten away from eating this kind of food.*
- *I'm on a diet, and I'd rather not have them in the house. It would just be too tempting.*

If the person insists that a little bit won't hurt you, keep repeating your response, and if necessary say, *I was hoping you'd respect my feelings about this. I prefer not to argue with you.*

## "Can You Do Me a Favor?": How to Say No

Doing helpful things for others is a very satisfying way of strengthening our human connections. It feels good to know we have the ability to make someone's life a little easier or more pleasant, and that the other person would do the same for us. Independent as we may be, all of us need to know there are people we can count on, even for something as simple as watering our plants when we're away. Most of the time we welcome opportunities to connect on a positive level with others and are happy to say yes when asked for assistance.

As long as doing the favor would cause you no major conflict or inconvenience, it's worth saying yes for a more practical reason, too: Your "good track record" will make it easier when you *do* want to say no. And when you feel confident that you're a person who is helpful and supportive of others in the larger sense, you're less likely to feel guilty about saying no in a specific situation.

## A Useful Technique

When life's obligations are piling up and you're reluctant to take on another one, saying no graciously can save you from overload. Here's a good technique for turning down any kind of inconvenient request. Begin with a phrase like "I'm sure you didn't realize this, but . . ." and then offer a piece of information that explains why you must say no. For example:

- *I'm sure you didn't realize this, but the slightest whiff of garlic makes me break out in hives. So I'm afraid I won't be able to run the kissing booth at the County Garlic Festival this year.*

The "revelation" (in this case, the fact that garlic gives you hives) may be something the person requesting the favor knows perfectly well. But by assuming he doesn't, you allow him to save face while you're rejecting his request. In effect, you're assuring him of your belief that had he only known the real situation, he would never have asked in the first place. In light of this, most people will accept your no response and not press the matter further. Another example:

- *You obviously didn't know this, but I'm in and out all day, so I can't promise I'll be here when your package arrives. I'm sure you'd rather arrange for someone else to accept your package.*

## Is This Your "Volunteer Work"?

Not all volunteer work takes place in soup kitchens and hospitals. At times the need for your help is closer to home, but you just don't realize it. People sometimes request favors because they've got no other options left. Requests can come from an elderly or sick neighbor, perhaps, or a struggling single mom at her wits' end.

If you're one of those people who is always meaning to do volunteer work but can never quite get around to it, your "mission" may be right under your nose. Before you figure out how to avoid getting involved with someone in need, think about whether helping this person in a conscious way might be something you want to do just because it's a good thing to do. That doesn't mean you have to be at their beck and call twenty-four hours a day. But you could make a secret commitment to give this person an hour or two of your time a week. Don't think of it as a chore. Think of it as your way of offering service to another human being. For an elderly neighbor, that could mean a standing date to run errands, help with paperwork, or just visit. For a single mom, it could mean offering to baby-sit one night a week while she goes to school.

At those times when you need to say no for one reason or another, any related guilt will be offset by the knowledge that you're making a difference in someone's life.

## Baby-sitting and Pet-sitting

We can't imagine a favor with more responsibility attached to it than agreeing to care for someone else's child. Looking after a beloved pet is a close second. If you would find it an imposition to have to care for someone else's child or pet, other people need to respect that. Remember that the most basic no's are often the most effective. A simple response such as *I'm afraid I can't* or *I'm not available* is all you're required to say and may be all you need. But if the other person doesn't accept that, or if you feel obliged to supply an excuse, try one of the following:

### Saying No When You'd Rather Not Be Asked Again

- *Unless it's an emergency, I have to say no. I'm afraid I'm not very good with children/animals.*
- *I know how much you love your cat, and I don't think I'm up to that kind of responsibility.*
- *My schedule's too erratic. I can't promise to be there when you need me.*
- *You obviously didn't know this, but my husband is terribly allergic to cats and dogs. So I'm afraid we can't look after Spike while you're out of town.*
- *I'm sorry I can't help you; I'm genuinely afraid of dogs/cats/snakes/quadruplets.*

If you can, suggest someone more appropriate. Don't think of it as passing the buck—think of it as offering a possible solution to the problem.

- *I'm afraid I can't. But Susan has kids around the same ages as yours. Maybe she'd be able to baby-sit.*
- *I'm afraid I can't. But Edith loves dogs. Maybe she'd be able to walk Rambo when you're away.*

Recommend a professional. Besides being a way to say no, it also reminds people that they should perhaps expect to pay for the kind of service they're asking you to do for free. (These responses will work even if the person offers you money.)

- *I'm sorry, I won't be able to baby-sit for the twins. I know Susan uses baby-sitters a lot. Why don't you ask her for a recommendation?*
- *Sorry, I won't be able to take Simba out to the park. I know there are some dog-walking services in the neighborhood. Have you tried them?*

**Saying No While Leaving the Door Open for the Future**

- *Not this time.*
- *Sorry, I won't be able to baby-sit. I have other plans.*
- *Sorry, I can't. This isn't a good day.*
- *I'm afraid I can't. This is going to be a very hectic weekend for me. I only want to take care of Charlie when I know I'll be able to give him plenty of attention. But please check with me next time.*

**Reversing a Pattern**

In some instances, a bad precedent has already been set, which will need to be addressed. If you've gotten into the habit of looking after your friend's children after school for free and are looking for a way out, it's not quite fair to do an abrupt reversal or start making excuses. You need to be more straightforward about what you want. Depending on your objective, here are some ways to break a pattern that's already taken hold:

- *I really enjoy watching your children, but it is a lot of work and a big responsibility. If you'd like me to continue caring for them, it's only fair that we work out some kind of compensation. Do you agree?*

If she agrees, say, *I've done some research about the going rate, and $___ a week seems fair. How does that sound?*

Of course, if she doesn't agree, tell her you'd like her to look for somebody else. And don't feel guilty—it's a tough job!

- *I don't want to leave you in the lurch, but I'm not going to be able to watch the children indefinitely. We can talk about the timing, but you're going to have to find someone else.*
- *When I started watching your kids after school, I didn't realize it would turn into an ongoing situation. They're great kids, but it's a big responsibility to have them in my care. I have to tell you that I can't commit to doing it much longer. I'd like you to make other arrangements for them.*

## Saying No to Working for Free

Often friends and relatives expect us to extend our professional services to them for free—whether it's medical care, legal counsel, haircuts, home or auto repair, writing, accounting, or anything else we normally get paid to do. While you may have no problem offering advice or doing a little unpaid labor, be ready to set limits if you're being pushed too far.

### Saying "No More Freebies"

- *I was happy to help you with your résumé, but it sounds like you have quite a few other projects in mind, too. I'm afraid I won't be able to help with all the alternate versions and the cover letters.* (Optional: *That is, unless you're willing to work on a client-consultant basis. In that case, I could give you a ten-percent discount off my usual rates.*)
- *When I started pruning your shrubbery, I was just starting out and had plenty of time. I also needed the experience. Now that my business has grown so much, I need to make my customers a priority. If you want me to continue, I'm going to have to start charging you. The rate would be _____.* (Optional: *I'm giving you my "Friends and Family Discount."*)
- *I'm very excited that you're almost done with your dissertation, and yes, I'd be happy to type it for you. I charge ____ an hour.* (Or: *I'll be able to give you a package rate after I look over the project and see how much is involved.*)
- *You know, I'm working so hard these days, that when I have time off, work is the last thing I want to think about. Why don't you make an appointment to see me in my office?*

### The Policy

A response like the following explaining your policy can be very useful. It lets people know that paying for your services gives them the right to make demands. Conversely, it conveys the message that if they don't expect to pay, they can't expect you to make their job a top priority. For example:

- *I have a policy about not working free for friends or relatives, and I'll tell you why. Home renovations can get pretty complicated. I want all my customers to be happy with what they get and have the right to complain if they're not happy. I've found that things work out much better for everyone when I treat each job as a business relationship.*

### Prevention

If you sense that someone's about to ask you for a consultation, free haircut, or other service, keep the request at bay with a preemptive statement such as:

- *I am so glad to be away from the office and to not have to think about other people's gastrointestinal problems for one night.*
- *Work has been so busy lately. The weekend was brutal. It's so good to know I won't have a pair of scissors in my hand again until Thursday.*

Some professionals—such as editors, agents, casting directors, record producers, or college admissions officers—are frequently sought out by hopefuls who want to win their support. If you're one of these powerful decision-makers, don't advertise yourself. Keep mum about it at parties if you want a night off from hearing pitches. When someone asks, "What do you do?" talk about your outside interests instead of work.

- *I love to dance; I play volleyball; I volunteer at a nursing home; I'm taking a French cooking class, and I'm really liking it. . . .*

Or respond with the classic:

- *As little as possible.*

## Trading Services

When people ask for your professional services as a favor—or in situations where you wouldn't be comfortable charging money—consider whether there's something they can do to help solve a problem for you. It's a friendly way to keep your relationship well balanced while you're taking care of business.

For some people, "trading favors" with friends solves problems and saves money. We know quite a few overburdened parents who have linked up with other parents and started baby-sitting co-ops. Mom and Dad get a night out, save a bundle on child care, and forge connections with other folks in similar situations.

Other trading situations we've heard about include:

- A Web designer who created a Web site for a caterer, who returned the favor with a few home-cooked dinners.
- A graphic designer who created a promotional brochure for an accountant, who prepared her tax return and offered financial-planning advice.
- A hair stylist who provided several free haircuts in exchange for carpentry work.

## "Don't Touch My Stuff!": How Not to Be a Lender

Many people are a little neurotic about lending out certain possessions. Maybe you are, too, if you've got an especially soft spot for your books, CDs, tools, clothing, car, or anything else. Some of us just don't want anybody else touching our stuff. What if they forget to return it? Or lose it? Or damage it? *That* would be a crisis.

Even when your reasons for not wanting to lend an item are perfectly valid, saying no to such a request implies that you don't trust the other person to get it back to you in good condition. To make your reluctance to lend seem less like a judgment on the other person's character, put the blame on yourself. Admit that maybe you *are* a little too attached to your Craftsman cordless drill or your vintage copy of *Beatles '65*. If you let it out of your grasp, you'd be worried sick. And that's why, crazy as it sounds, you're afraid you just can't lend it. Here are some ways to protect your prized possessions:

### Your Wheels

- *I'm a little crazy when it comes to my car. I'm just not comfortable letting anybody else drive it. Sorry.*
- *I know you're a good driver, but it's different when it's my car. I'd worry too much. If anything went wrong, I'd feel terrible—like I was responsible somehow. So I have to say no.*

### Books

- *The Policy: I'm one of those people who hates parting with the books I love. I just need to know they're around and that I can read them anytime. That's why I have a policy of never lending them out.*
- *There are some books I'm very attached to, and this is one of them. I pick it up and read from it quite often. So I'd rather not lend it out.*
- *Actually, I was planning to read this again soon, so I don't want to lend it out.* (Optional: *But I love this one so much, let me buy you a copy. I'd really like to do that, and then we can talk about it together. Or: But this is such a classic, I'm pretty sure you'll be able to find a copy at the library.*)

### CDs, Records, Tapes, Videos, Etc.

- The Policy: *It's my policy not to lend out CDs/records/tapes. If I get an urge to listen to certain music and then it's not there, I go nuts.*
- *I don't want to lend this CD/record/tape out because I play it all the time.*

- *I'd rather not lend out the video, but why don't you come over one night and we'll watch it together?*

## Tools

- *Sorry, I don't lend my tools out, because I never know when I'll need them.* (Optional: *But I could bring it over next Saturday and help you with your repairs.*)

## Clothing, Jewelry, Accessories:

- *I know you'd be very careful, but I'd feel terrible if anything happened to this necklace. It's got a lot of sentimental value for me. I'm really not comfortable lending it. I'm sure you'll understand.*
- *I trust you more than most people, but I've had too many bad experiences with lending out clothes to friends. It's probably safer for both of us if I don't lend it to you.*

## Anything

- *You know that saying, "Neither a borrower nor a lender be"? I've always considered it very good advice for staying out of trouble and preserving friendships—which is why I have to say no!*

## Giving Rides and Going Shopping

We're all for carpooling and reducing the number of vehicles on the road. But it can become inconvenient when someone asks you for a ride and it means having to wait around or go significantly out of your way. Requests to pick up something at the store are similar—sometimes it's easy to help out, sometimes it's not.

Please say yes as often as you can—and not just for environmental reasons. Accommodating someone with a ride when it's not too inconvenient makes it easier to say no at other times. When those times occur, try one of the following:

- *I'm happy to drive you there, but I can't wait for you because I've got one errand to run. So if you don't mind taking a cab/the bus home, I can drop you off.*
- *I can take you as far as the Grove Street Station, but then I have to veer off toward Maplewood. I'm afraid I don't have time today to drop you off at the mall.*
- *Sorry, I can't. This is really a bad day.* (Optional: *I'll probably have some free time on Wednesday, though, if you can wait till then.)*
- *I'll be glad to get your groceries when I go to the supermarket tomorrow. But I can't go now.* (Optional: *If you need milk today, I can give you some.)*
- *It really wouldn't be convenient today. I've got a million stops to make.* (Optional: *I don't know what time I'll get back later, but if you need me to pick something up, I'd be glad to.)*

While it's often difficult to say no to family and friends, keep in mind that sometimes it's the best thing you can do for your relationship. When you feel free to set limits—whether to claim time for yourself or defend yourself against impositions—you feel less resentful and more generous toward the important people in your life. Though you may disappoint one another from time to time, you'll be in better shape to weather each storm when your heart isn't burdened by accumulated anger.

Especially in the midst of turmoil with loved ones, it helps to remember that we are blessed to have people who care about us and want us in their lives.

# 6 Saying No to Kids

. . . . . . . . . . . . . . . . . . . . . . . . . . . . . . . . . . . . . . . . . . . . . . . . . . . . . . . . . . . . . . . . . . . .

*When it comes to my kids, no matter how much I do, I always feel like I should be doing* more.

—Mother of two young children

*I let my son drop out of high school; I knew he was hanging out with a bad crowd. I always had a hard time saying no to him. I think it was because I hated to see him unhappy.*

—Divorced father of a grown son

*Sometimes out of guilt I'll buy him more things than I might ordinarily, because I feel bad about not spending more time with him.*

—Mother of a six-year-old boy

For some parents, saying no to their children is the hardest "no" of all. As a result, their kids are rarely denied. Whether it's the latest action figure, a new privilege, or the right to interrupt Mom at will, the demands of these children are usually met.

Virtually all parenting experts agree that children need firm, clear boundaries in order to learn appropriate behavior and to grow into reasonable, responsible adults. Very few parents would disagree, at least in theory. So why do so many have difficulty setting limits and saying no to their children? Here are some of the most common reasons:

1. *It's easier (at least for the moment).* Parents often say yes to kids because they want to avoid conflict. Telling a child he can't have what he wants is not going to please him. And children are much more likely than adults to express their displeasure in very displeasing ways—like screaming "I hate you!" and pounding their fists on the wall. (Of course, some grown-ups are also capable of this.) When you're tired and short on patience to begin with, it's very tempting to cave in just to keep the peace. *Sure, sweetie. Eat the whole bag of marshmallows. Just do it quietly.* As one mother put it, " 'Yes' ends the discussion. 'No' continues the discussion."

   Giving in on little things is no big deal, and probably a necessary tactic for surviving day-to-day family life. However, while saying yes may buy you momentary peace, teaching children to hear and accept "no" is a better investment that promotes more lasting harmony.

2. *We want to be liked/loved.* Raising children is such a tough job, you really can't blame yourself for wanting plenty of appreciation in return. It feels so gratifying when children express their love and affection. It's a lot less fun when they're accusing you of being mean and horrible. In her book *Loving Your Child Is Not Enough*, parent educator Nancy Samalin notes that many parents fall into "The Happiness Trap." Says Samalin, "If our need to keep children happy and loving toward us is too compelling, we will find it impossible to say no to them." But catering to your child's desires all the time is not in her best interest, nor in yours.

3. *We feel guilty saying no.* You don't have to be a working mother to worry that you're not giving your child enough time and attention (though it helps). Many parents we spoke to admitted that they struggle with occasional guilt and compensate by indulging their children, either by giving more presents or allowing more privileges.

Like the first mother quoted at the beginning of this chapter, you may feel that whatever effort you make on your child's behalf, no matter how much time you spend together, it's never enough. This may make it difficult to say no when your child demands your undivided attention, regardless of what else you might be doing. (Are you the kind of parent who is unable to utter a sentence like "Just a minute, I'm on the phone"?) But teaching kids that you're not going to drop everything whenever they summon you doesn't deprive them of yourself. It cultivates good manners, respect for others, and reinforces the lesson that we sometimes have to wait for gratification. Learning to be patient helps prepare children to tolerate life's inevitable frustrations.

4. *We fear that saying no will deprive them of a special experience.* "Kids will always tell you, 'But, Mom, everybody else is doing it,'" says Deborah Carroll, author of *Teaching Your Children Life Skills...While Having a Life of Your Own.* "Sometimes they can get you wondering whether you're making a mistake as a parent. But you have to recognize that this is an age-old tactic, and learn to trust your own judgment."

While your child may rail against the restrictions you impose, that doesn't mean you're doing the wrong thing. And it doesn't mean your child will turn against you. Just as we have finally forgiven our mothers for not letting us go to Woodstock, your child will most likely come around to respecting you for doing your job as a parent. And if you're lucky, it won't take thirty years.

5. *Personal history gets in the way.* Those who were raised in very strict, authoritarian homes might feel strongly that "I'm not going to be like my parents" or "My kids aren't going to go through what I went through." In his book *If You Had Controlling Parents,* family therapist Dan Neuharth, Ph.D., notes, "If you were raised with too much control, you may

unwittingly react by raising your children with insufficient limits or control."

Other issues may come into play as well. One woman we know, who lost her parents at an early age and spent part of her childhood in an orphanage, told us she rarely said no to her son out of fear that she might somehow lose him. As long as she could keep him happy, she reasoned, he would stick around.

As we'll see, parents who can't say no are shortchanging their kids *and* themselves.

## Why Saying No Is Positive Parenting

When children are very young, you first say no to protect them from danger. As they begin to crawl and explore, you must teach them not to touch the stove or climb up where they can hurt themselves. As they get a little older, you teach them not to play with matches, not to run into the street, and not to talk to strangers. Of course, you don't say no to be mean. You say it because you love your child and because you must teach him to protect himself.

Just as saying no is a tool to help ensure your child's physical safety, it also contributes to his emotional security. When you set limits on your child's behavior, whether it's telling a five-year-old he can't hit the baby or telling a teenager he can't stay out past midnight, you're letting him know that his actions don't happen in a vacuum. He's connected to someone (you) who watches and cares what he does. All children need a safe space in which to grow and develop. While it's a child's nature to test the limits of that space, by climbing higher, venturing farther, or asking for more of what he wants, it's also comforting for him to know he's not out there alone.

In his book *Parenting by Heart*, Dr. Ron Taffel refers to this safe space as the "empathic envelope," which acts like a container around children. Says Taffel, "Theoretically, as the parent, you are in charge of this container. It is made up of *your* values, *your* expectations, and *your* ways of being with your children. . . . It gives them a sense that they *belong* somewhere, that they are *held* by their parents in a safe and secure place: 'This is my house. I know what to expect. I belong.'"

It's impossible to establish those comforting boundaries for children without saying no. That all-important little word needs to be part of your vocabulary if you want your child to feel secure and connected. In a loving context, saying no is a loving act. It provides children with guideposts for appropriate behavior that they will carry forward as they grow. If you have difficulty saying it because you dread the conflict that may result or because you feel guilty depriving your child of something she desperately wants, it's important to remember that parents and kids aren't *supposed* to agree on everything. If they do, something's probably wrong. To do your job well as a parent, you sometimes have to be the bad guy.

Family therapist Jodi Conway has worked with many parents who were unable to establish adequate limits, and notes the effects this has on children. "Believe it or not," she says, "a child who is brought up without boundaries is a terrified child. It's a very scary feeling to know that at age five, you are the boss of the house. These children feel like they're out of control. They often have a hard time coping in school, completing work, and dealing with people."

## Preparing for the Road Ahead

Saying no is not simply a means of applying controls to your child's behavior in the here and now. It's a way of instilling a sense of *self-control* that she will carry through her entire life. This is one of the most important lessons parents can teach their children, and it becomes increasingly important as kids grow. The investment you make by setting limits and teaching appropriate behavior to your child will pay off enormously when she hits adolescence.

As kids get bigger, the stakes get higher. All too soon, they will be confronting issues like drugs, drinking, driving, and sex. It's enough to make your parental heart quake. Much as you might like to lock them in their rooms for their own protection, obviously you can't. And much as you want to monitor their movements around the clock, you won't always know where they are and whom they're with. There will be situations you're not aware of. Your fifteen-year-old daughter probably isn't going to call you from a party to ask, "Mom, this cute nineteen-year-old guy just invited me to drive out to the lake with him, and he's had about eleven beers so far. Can I go?"

Your teenager will have to make many choices that affect her safety and well-being. As she navigates these difficult, confusing years, the best protection she can have is her own good judgment. The firm, caring guidance you provide as she's growing—by saying no to behavior you want to discourage—helps cultivate her good judgment and provides a model for making smart, appropriate choices.

"We're asking kids to say no to a lot of things these days," says author Deborah Carroll, the parent of three teenagers. "But if we don't teach them by example, how will they ever learn to say it themselves? If we don't show them that saying no is normal and acceptable, how can we expect them to suddenly 'get it' when they're older and someone is offering them drugs for the first time?"

In the words of family therapist Dr. Dan Neuharth, "With too little control, we give our children no blueprint and no signposts with which they can navigate the world. They will have to learn about life and its limits from others, who may not be the best role models."

By saying no when kids are young, you lay the groundwork for a smoother ride through the tumultuous adolescent years.

## Short-Term Pain, Long-Term Gain

*A couple we're friendly with could never say no to their daughter. If the adults were sitting and talking and she came in, the parents would turn away from their guests and give her their full attention. They would never let her know that this was grown-up time. It drove us crazy. One day this child, five years old, screamed at her mother, "I'm going to kill you!" The parents got scared and took her to a therapist, who said, "You've got to give her some boundaries." They worked with her. And eventually this demon child turned out to be a lovely little girl.*

—Mother of a toddler

The most successful parents we know assure us that while blow-ups are inevitable, the long-term dividends of saying no to kids make the bumpy times well worth enduring. Despite the pouting and protests you're bound to face, establishing firm, clear guidelines for appropriate behavior sets the stage for a happier, more peaceful household over time.

In families where children don't seem to respect limits, the real cause may be parents' inability to say no and stick to it. Family therapist Paula Solomon, who leads parenting workshops in Brooklyn, New York, says that many of the parents she sees fit this description.

"They'll come to me and say they're frustrated," says Solomon. "Their child is extremely demanding and unreasonable; he's refusing to go to bed, finding any number of ways to prolong staying up, asking for one more cookie, one more toy, one more story. When I begin to ask specific questions, it becomes clear that the parents are not saying no consistently and firmly to the child's stalling tactics. I make very practical suggestions about how they can solve the problem, but often they just can't do it. They'll say, 'I feel terrible, like I'm depriving him. I need to be available. I can't stand to hear him cry. I feel like a bad parent.' These things tell me it's a limit-setting issue.

It's not that their child is doing anything so outrageous or over the top. More often it's the parents' problem."

For the objectionable behavior to improve, says Solomon, these parents need to put their own guilt on the back burner, say no, and not back down. Because children take comfort from rituals and rules, she suggests using a kitchen timer as part of the bedtime routine to make the process easier. "Parents need to say, 'No more. You have to stay in bed. You can read for ten minutes, but when the timer goes off, it's lights out. That's the rule.' "

For the rules to make a difference, parents must be able to enforce them. It may be difficult at first, but it will pay off.

## Today's Spoiled Child . . . Tomorrow's Spoiled Adult

*My ten-year-old niece was sitting on the sofa watching TV, and my sister brought her an ice-cream cone with sprin-kles. A nice treat, right? Instead of saying thank you, Anna whined. She didn't want* rainbow *sprinkles, she wanted* chocolate *sprinkles! So what did my sister do? She took the cone back into the kitchen, scraped off the rainbow sprinkles, and gave her chocolate sprinkles. I wanted to scream!*

—Concerned aunt

Should we blame Anna for whining and demanding a new-and-improved ice-cream cone? She only does it because it works.

It may be true that parents are having a harder time saying no these days, but the inability to set limits with kids is certainly nothing new. The evidence for this is everywhere. Just look around your neighborhood or your office, for example: All of us are surrounded by selfish, spoiled former children. The boss from hell who rants and raves to get what he wants. The prima donna co-worker who expects you to drop everything for her. The guy next door washing his car with the stereo blasting loud enough to blow away half the block.

It helps to think of people like this next time you feel your-self, against your better judgment, caving in to your child's demands. In your adult life, you don't like dealing with people who expect everything to go their way, who can't accept dis-appointment or see another's point of view. Then why would you want to raise another one?

If the situation between Anna and her mother is typical of their usual interactions (and according to our spy, it is), Anna may be well on her way to becoming one of these not-too-delightful ex-children. Anna's mom is not doing her daughter any favors by catering to her every whim. Here, she is missing a perfect opportunity to help Anna learn several things: a) to express thanks when someone gives her a special treat, b) to ac-cept that she will not always get exactly what she wants, c) to take responsibility (e.g., by going to the kitchen and getting the chocolate sprinkles herself), and d) respect for her mother.

Giving your child age-appropriate responsibilities teaches her about give-and-take and increases the odds that she will grow into a reasonable adult rather than a self-centered pill. Looking ahead through the years, which would *you* rather have in your immediate family?

As one woman told us, "I have a forty-five-year-old cousin who always got her way by throwing a fit. And she *still* throws fits!"

## Finding the Right Balance

Some people have an instinctive aversion to words like "lim-its," "boundaries," and "control." They equate these words with others like "stifling" and "repressive." As parents, they fear that imposing restrictions on their child will inhibit his imagination and destroy creativity. "Why would I want to limit my child?" they ask. "I want him to know no boundaries!"

To this we respond: Was Shakespeare's creativity limited by the strict meter of a sonnet? Were the Japanese poets displaying a lack of imagination when they wrote in haiku form?

The fact is, structure is not the enemy of creativity, and there's a big difference between imposing limits on a child's behavior and limiting his potential as a human being. "Free rein" does not equal "free spirit." Quite the opposite: Parents who give kids an overdose of freedom are promoting confusion, not creativity.

"I see a lot of parents who give their kids too much freedom and too many choices before they're old enough to handle them," says therapist Paula Solomon. "They'll walk into a bakery and say, 'Okay, what do you want?' and then suggest everything in the store. The child is completely overwhelmed. She has no idea what she wants. They could be in there forever!"

On the other hand, offering two choices ( "Do you want a raisin muffin or an apple muffin?") gives her a manageable framework in which to exercise her freedom of choice. And if she says, "Neither . . . I want a bagel," that's fine, too. She's just expanded her options at her own comfortable rate.

## Dealing with Doubts and Guilt

*You want to be fair; you want to do the right thing. But I have this vision of my daughter sitting on a couch in twenty years, talking to a psychiatrist about some terrible thing I did to her.*

—Mother of two school-age children

More than one parent we spoke to was haunted by a similar image of her child's future psychiatric treatment! It's almost as if self-doubt is an occupational hazard of parenthood. For parents who understand the importance of saying no to children, the nagging question is "How do I know where to draw the line? Are my 'firm, loving guidelines' overly harsh?

When my kids accuse me of being a tyrant, how do I know they're not right—at least *this* time?"

Since parenting is not an exact science, it's very possible you *will* sometimes make a decision that later seems overly strict. That doesn't mean you've done irreparable damage or that your children will resent you for the rest of their lives. Dr. Dan Neuharth advises parents worried about maintaining balanced discipline to focus on the big picture rather than on the small details.

"There is a wide range of acceptable parenting between too little control and too much," says Neuharth. "All parents make mistakes. But virtually no single controlling action and no single lapse in control will have lasting consequences. If you can be sure your child feels loved, appreciated, and part of the family, then over time, these feelings will overshadow any single episode of over-control or under-control."

When you begin to doubt your own judgment and your resolve begins to crumble, it helps to have someone who can act as a sounding board—or cheer you on. In this way, parents can support each other.

"My friend and I have been there for each other since our kids were born three months apart," says the mother of a teenager. "I'd call her in the middle of a fight with my daughter and say, 'She's in her room having a temper tantrum! I need to talk to you!' My friend would give me a pep talk and say, 'You did the right thing. Don't go in there. It'll blow over.'"

It can also be useful to network with other parents to find out whether, in fact, "all the other kids are doing it." A little research into what other parents permit can give you some perspective on issues like curfews. (Don't do this in your child's presence, though; it will embarrass her in a big way.) But remember that *you* are the final judge of what's best for your child, and you're free to deviate from the pack if the prevailing views make you uncomfortable. For example, we were surprised recently when a friend told us that among parents of teenagers in her area, underage drinking at home is widely tolerated. The rationale is that the kids are going to do it anyway, so we might as well provide them with a safe environment in which to do it. Our friend and her husband think this is a bad idea all around—not to mention illegal—and have made that crystal clear to their own teenagers.

## Don't Give in to Little Guilt-Mongers

As every parent knows, children can be masters of manipulation. To get what they want, they'll pull every string and press every button at their disposal. They'll say things like "You're mean," "You don't love me," "I wish I could go live at Stephanie's house." Words like these can make some parents crumble with guilt. And if kids succeed in getting their way with these guilt-mongering tactics, they'll use them again and again.

At such times, advises author and workshop leader Nancy Samalin, "Parents need not to melt. They need to say, 'I don't blame you for being mad, but this is still what I expect.' Guilt is a very useless emotion when it comes to raising kids."

In the meantime, if your little guilt-monger manages to hit a nerve and undermine your confidence about saying no, steel yourself. Feel guilty if you must, but hang tough. You just need a bit of practice. Showing kids that their guilt-tripping has no effect on you will take away their incentive for doing it.

Working with her therapy clients, says Jodi Conway, "I tell parents in the beginning, 'If you feel guilty, that's the first sign you're doing the right thing. That lets you know you've said no.' The guilt wears off after a while."

## Teenagers: Changing the Rules

In the best-case scenario, parents say no to their children consistently and firmly from the beginning. As a reward for their efforts, the kids evolve according to plan, growing into reasonably responsible, trustworthy teenagers. But what if you haven't, and they're not?

Despite what anyone tells you, it's never too late (though it *is* much harder). Don't throw up your hands and surrender. Instead, resolve to change the rules and start setting limits in a more conscientious way. But let your kids know there's a new game in town. You could even make a preemptive announcement and say something like:

- *Up till now I've given you a lot of latitude. I've taken a pretty laid-back approach. But now that you're older, things are more serious; there are more potential dangers out there. Because I love you and care about you, I want to make sure I'm involved in the choices you make and that you know where I stand. So we're going to change the way things are around here. I'll always try to be fair with you. But you're probably going to hear me say no more often than I have before.*

Emphasize that while they may not like some of the restrictions you impose, you expect your decisions to be respected.

You're bound to hear a lot of protests, and you'll need a lot of resolve and determination to hold your ground. But ultimately your child will benefit if you play a more active role. Says one mother of teenagers, "Kids like knowing you're paying attention. They like knowing someone cares, even if they say they don't. The ones who have total freedom may tell you they love it, but they don't. They feel like nobody gives a damn."

## In the Thick of It: Saying No to Kids

*No. Because I said so.*
*No. Because I'm your mother/father, that's why.*
*I'm sorry, you can't do that. My house, my rules.*

Sound familiar? In some ways, these lines are as classic as anything out of Shakespeare. Parents have been reciting them for generations, and chances are yours did, too. Perhaps it's not the most sophisticated way of communicating, but it leaves little room for doubt about how Mom or Dad feels regarding the matter at hand. Confusion is averted; clarity prevails. Let's face it: Phrases like these come in very handy from time to time.

Many parents, when they say no, feel the need to justify their decision to their child with elaborate explanations. They babble on way too long and supply a lot more information than is necessary. When it's time for the kids to turn off the television, they might say something like, "I don't want you to watch anymore TV today because those cartoon programs are so mindless and way too violent and I'm afraid you'll begin to think that dropping an anvil on someone's head is an appropriate way of resolving differences, and besides, the more time you spend glued to the tube, the less time you'll spend doing something creative or educational or even going outside and playing in the fresh air and getting exercise, which is a very healthy habit you should start right now if you want to stay in shape when you're older."

Whew! By now the kids' eyes have glazed over—and not from the cartoons.

Children *do* deserve to know why you're saying no. It helps them make sense of why you're steering their behavior in a particular direction. It's also part of the way you pass on your values to them. But explanations need to be appropriate for a child's age and presented in a way he can absorb. In the above case, for example, the parent may wish to offer the kids a reason they're not allowed to keep watching TV. But one reason at a time is plenty. More is overkill. And if the parent meets resistance, she shouldn't hesitate to end the discussion with a classic line like "Because that's the rule." Citing a rule is an effective tool of discipline, because young children respect rules and appreciate the structure they provide.

With young children especially, the more you talk, the less you'll be heard. One mother told us, "My four-year-old is very clear. If I start to use too many words to explain, he'll say, 'Don't talk, Mommy.' He's overloaded! He's letting me know that he's not taking it in."

Depending on your child's age, a simple "That's enough TV for now" or "Time to put the toys away" may be all you need. Why? Because you said so.

Overexplaining to children can also lead you into the same trap you face when you overexplain to adults: The more you talk, the less decisive you appear and the more openings you provide for the other person to argue the point. And once they sense an opening, kids charge right in ("But, Mom, I played kickball with my friends for a whole hour this morning and I got a *lot* of exercise already. Shouldn't I be allowed to relax for a while?").

Keeping it simple leaves you on stabler ground.

Within families, every day holds the potential for a great many differences of opinion. Which means that parents may be called upon to invoke the word "no" in a wide variety of situations, including those requiring that popular variation on the "no" theme, "Don't do that!"

While we can't begin to address all these situations, we have put together some all-purpose guidelines.

## 11 Tips for Saying No to Kids

The following tips are all useful, but think of the first two as *supreme commandments.*

### 1. Be consistent

You've heard this before, but it's *the* number-one rule of saying no to children. "No" means nothing to your child if you say yes five minutes later. When you waffle and relent to stop his whining or nagging, you throw away an opportunity to teach him the meaning of the word—and make your life easier in the future. Instead, caving in teaches him that your "no" can be overturned on appeal. The next time you say it, he'll keep at you until you give in again.

Being consistent doesn't mean that you can never change your mind about an issue. Of course you can. While some "no's" are nonnegotiable (e.g., no hitting the baby), others are not-this-time "no's," such as "No, you can't stay up late tonight." If you're not sure how you feel, buy time by telling your child you need to think it over. But once you've made your decision, stick to it.

### 2. Establish a system of consequences

This used to be called "punishment." Maybe it's just semantics, but we prefer the new term because it comes closer to the idea of parent as an authoritative but caring teacher as opposed to a prison warden. Call it what you will; the bottom line is, you can't effectively say no to your child if he believes there are no consequences for misbehavior.

Parents who feel guilty saying no to their children will probably have trouble applying consequences, but the two are inseparable, and equally important. When you say no to your child, the prospect of consequences gives your words credibility and weight. They tell him, "What you do matters. I care about the choices you make." They're part of what creates that safe space where your child feels connected to someone and protected by boundaries. It's your love in action, slightly disguised.

The ability to follow through with consequences is an essential part of being consistent. With young children, you could impose a time-out or remove a favorite toy for a while. For older kids, it could mean being grounded or deprived of a privilege like TV, computer, phone time, or use of the car.

### 3. Make eye contact

Before you say a word, ensure that you have your child's full attention. If necessary, turn off the TV, or ask her to turn away from the computer or put down the toy she's playing with.

### 4. Tell, don't ask

Unless you're playing *Jeopardy!* with your kids, there's no need to phrase things in the form of a question. When speaking to your child, watch your voice: Does it go up at the end of the sentence—you know, like this? If so, concentrate on speaking in a confident, decisive tone. When you say, "Do you want to eat your dinner now?" or "Pick up your clothes, okay?" you're asking for an argument.

### 5. Keep explanations simple and age-appropriate

Mommies and Daddies are entitled to expect certain behavior without having to justify themselves.

### 6. Don't be afraid to repeat yourself

This essential tactic applies when dealing with adults as well as children. When another person, old or young, is having trouble accepting that "no means no," you are not required to come up with new ways to explain your decision. Once you've told your son, "I don't want you owning a BB gun because someone could get hurt," there's really nothing else you need to say. If he persists in arguing, repeat yourself a few times, using essentially the same language. Then let him know the case is closed.

### 7. Acknowledge feelings—then move on

Most parenting experts recommend that when a child is upset, parents actively acknowledge the child's feelings to let her know that she is being heard and understood. That makes sense: Everyone wants to feel that her own reality matters. Acknowledging feelings should also be part of the process of saying no.

If your child is angry or disappointed because you've denied her something she wants, you might be tempted to try to lessen the impact by saying, "It's not such a big deal" or "There's no reason to be so angry." But this will likely just make things worse. Instead, be sympathetic to her feelings, but don't dwell on them. It's enough to say, "I see that you're angry, and I'm sorry you feel that way, but I really don't want you to have that now. If you can calm down and control yourself, you can have it later." The fact is, the two of you *are* at odds. It's best to recognize that and move on.

### 8. Don't belittle

Saying no is meant to guide your child's behavior, not to make him feel terrible or stupid. Don't demean him or ridicule him for wanting what he wants. Keep the focus of your "no" on the action, not the person. For example, saying, "One piece of cake is enough. You can have another piece tomorrow," is an appropriate way to limit dessert. Saying, "You want *another* piece? I can't believe what a pig you are!" is degrading.

### 9. Strive for a united front

When one parent says no and the other says yes, nobody wins. It sends your child confusing messages and invites her to manipulate the situation by "dividing and conquering." Divorced parents may have to struggle especially hard to present a united front, but try to resolve any disagreements away from your child. If necessary, buy time before responding to your child's request ("I want to talk it over with your dad first, and then we'll let you know"). If you simply don't agree, decide with your spouse or ex that you'll take turns being the decision-maker, or let the parent prevail who feels most strongly about a particular issue.

### 10. Expect cooperation

When you're saying no or trying to encourage certain behavior, don't anticipate problems before they occur (e.g., "We have to leave the house in ten minutes, and you're always making us late, so don't dawdle this time"). Instead, promote cooperation with a positive remark, like "I know you can do it" or "I'll bet a big girl like you can eat breakfast and put on her shoes in ten minutes flat." Set the bar at an achievable level, and remind her what she *can* do. She'll probably want to please you.

### 11. Be a model parent

(Easy to say, a lot harder to do.) For some people, having a child is a catalyst for cleaning up their act: They quit smoking, watch their language, and so on. But there are other forms of "bad behavior" grown-ups tend to indulge in that can be the very kind of behavior they scold their children for: rudeness and gossip, for example.

When you make cutting, sarcastic remarks to your spouse or say cruel things about other people, be aware that someone small is listening and learning from you. That doesn't mean you should repress anger or other perfectly natural emotions. It means you need to honestly size up your own behavior against the standard you want your children to live up to and resolve to be a good role model. Kind, respectful children learn from kind, respectful parents. You'll have less bad behavior to say no to if you don't flaunt it yourself.

## A Bag of Tricks for Parents

Here are some tools you can use to say no to kids in a wide range of situations. Remember: In order for them to work, you must apply them with *consistency and conviction!*

Some examples are geared toward young children, but most of these approaches can be customized for different ages.

### Invoke "The Family Policy"

Here we adapt one of our basic naysaying techniques for family use. The "Family Policy," like "House Rules," formalizes whatever practices or behavior you'd like to reinforce with your children. Unlike other rules that may change depending on the situation, the Family Policy is an absolute rule that applies 100 percent of the time. It tells your kids, "This is how we as a family behave; this is how we want to live." You can invoke your Family Policy as a more positive way of saying no. For example:

- *Our Family Policy is that we share our toys with friends when they come to visit.*
- *Our Family Policy is to have healthy snacks at home, so we don't keep soda and candy in the house.*
- *Hitting is against our Family Policy. It's not allowed, ever.*

### Prevention

Prepare your child in advance for situations in which you will most likely have to set limits. Adopt a positive tone ("This is what we're going to do"), rather than anticipating misbehavior ("Don't annoy me when Aunt Laura comes over"). Not a foolproof tactic (what is?), but it can help.

- *We're going to the supermarket now. Here's our list for today. This is all we're going to buy. You might see other stuff along the way that you'll want, but we're only going to get what's on the list.*

  *Later you can say, Remember I told you what we were going to buy today? That isn't on our list.*
- *We're going to the mall, but today is just a looking day. Another time we'll have a buying day and get something for you.*

By using this preventive tactic, you're inviting your child to make an agreement with you. That's why it's quite appropriate to ask "Okay?" or "Is it a deal?" when you tell her what you expect. But when the time comes to enforce your terms, don't ask questions. Be authoritative.

- *I have to make an important phone call, so I'll need a little time without being interrupted. I'll let you know when I'm finished and then we can talk. Is it a deal?*
- *When Joe and Cindy come tonight, we'll have a half hour of visiting time with you, and then the grown-ups want to visit with each other. So after a half hour, it's bedtime, okay?*

  Later on, remind your child of your agreement: *We had a*

*nice half hour together, and now it's bedtime. Say good night, everybody!*

Prevention is the best way to restrict the amount of time kids spend numbing their minds on TV and video games. Encourage them to be selective by setting a realistic cap on daily tube time.

- *When your homework's done, you can pick two shows to watch. What do you want to see? . . . Okay, and when the shows are over, the TV goes off.*

Other preventive tactics:
- Rent, don't buy, video-game players and cartridges. Use them on holidays or occasions when you want the kids out of your hair.
- Tape favorite shows to watch at convenient times. The ability to fast-forward through commercials is a big plus here.
- This might seem impossibly radical, but there's no law that says you *must* own a television. Some families actually do get by without them. At the very least, don't place a TV in your child's room. Not only is it more difficult to monitor his viewing, it also discourages family interaction and encourages your child to isolate himself.

### Buy Time

Taking time to think about how you really feel is preferable to making a quick decision you might later regret. It enables you to say no (or yes) with more conviction. Children will respect your decision, even if they don't like it.

- *I'm not sure I want you to stay over at Robbie's house tonight. Let me think about it, and I'll let you know later.*

### Turn the Tables

Parents often find themselves saying no to the same things over and over again. Kids being kids, they'll test and push and prod even when precedent makes it pretty obvious you're going to say no. For example, let's say your son repeatedly asks you to buy computer games that you feel are too graphic or violent. Next time he asks you for one, turn his question around and ask:

*What do* you *think I'm going to say?*

You can even ask him:

*And* why *do you think I don't want you to play games like that?*

In a sense, you're inviting him to play the role of you. He'll probably still give you an argument, but this tactic reinforces your values by getting him to acknowledge what you've already told him on previous occasions. It also lets you sound less like a broken record stuck in the "no" groove.

### Offer an Alternative

Suggesting a substitute for what your child wants puts a quick positive spin on your "no." It helps avert scenes by giving her *some* satisfaction, but on your terms. Make sure you stick to those terms and don't back down, or your child may trap you into endless, ongoing negotiations.

- *You can't stay up and watch another video, but I will read you an extra story tonight.*
- *I don't want you to have that because you've had enough junk today. If you're hungry, you can have an apple or a banana. Which would you like?*

### Tie Behavior to Privileges

- *Watching TV is a privilege, not a right. You don't earn the privilege until you finish your homework.*
- *It's actually very simple, Nicky. You feed and walk the dog, and then you can go out with your friends. So until Sparky gets his chow and his exercise, your pals will have to wait.*

Teenagers respond well to rewards and even written contracts. Specify what you expect them to do and what they will get in return for this behavior. (It's not bribery; it's the way of

169

the world.) Of course, if they don't hold up their end of the bargain, all bets are off.

- *I can't let you stay out past curfew for the party this weekend because you didn't pick up your brother from school like you promised. A deal's a deal, and you let me down.*
- *We had an agreement that you could go skiing with Randy's family over the holidays if you maintained a B average. So unless you can bring your grades up this semester, it looks like you'll be here with us instead.*

### "Earn It!"

Instead of saying no (or yes) outright, seize the chance to encourage responsibility and independence.

- *I'm not going to buy you that today, but you can buy it for yourself. Let's talk about how you can save from your allowance/earn the money you need.*
- *You can get a car if you help pay for it. I've noticed there are plenty of "help wanted" signs up at the mall. Get a job, and then we'll talk.*

### "Okay for Them, Not Okay for You"

It's virtually certain that on occasion your child will try to change your mind about something by noting that other parents allow it or other kids get away with it. There's only one good answer to this argument: "So be it." Here are a few variations on that theme:

- *It's irrelevant to me whether Jackson's mother lets him eat in his room. In this house we're only allowed to eat in the kitchen or dining room. So that bowl of chili needs to be taken into the kitchen.*
- *I know that Mommy lets you eat fried chicken for dinner at home, but I'm a vegetarian. That means I don't have meat in my house. On weekends when you're with me, I want you to eat this way, too. When you're older, you'll be able to choose which way you want to eat all the time.*
- *Maybe you hear other kids saying things like that, but we*

*don't talk about people that way in this family. It's bad manners, and it hurts people.*

- *It's true, adults do it all the time. But there's a difference between being an adult and being a kid. It's not appropriate for you.*

- *I don't care if everyone is going camping in the mountains this weekend. And maybe I am a neurotic, overprotective mother. But with no adult supervision, I don't want you going. And that's that.*

### After You've Said No: Facing the Storm

The toughest part of saying no is holding your ground in the face of a screaming, pouting, crying, or guilt-mongering child. The best formula includes acknowledging your child's feelings while repeating your decision and making it clear you have no intention of wavering. For example:

- *Maybe you're right. Maybe I am a dictator. But I do not feel comfortable letting you go to that party. I would be much too worried. I'm sorry you're angry, but my decision is final.*

- *You think I'm a clueless mother. Well, so be it. I use my best judgment, and we're not always going to agree. In my judgment, nine is way too young for a Wonderbra—so forget about it!*

In the heat of anger, it's easy to say or do something you might regret later. So when tempers are flaring—yours or your child's—leave the room yourself until you both cool down a bit.

- *I'm sorry you're mad at me. I hope you won't stay mad too long. Come and see me when you can talk without saying mean things.*

### Classic Conversation-Enders

Employed by generations of parents (including ours), these chestnuts are still valid and useful. Utter them in a determined tone of voice to tell your child, "This discussion is over!"

- *No, you can't. I don't care what the other kids are doing. If they all jumped off the Empire State Building, would you do it, too?*
- *Life isn't fair.*
- *"No" is a complete sentence.*
- *When you're grown up and living on your own, you can do whatever you like. Till then, I'm in charge.*
- *No ifs, ands, or buts!*
- *This is not a democracy.*

## The Ultimate Reward: "I Like These People!"

One mother we spoke to, who taught school for ten years before having her first child, said that exposure to many different children was a real eye-opener.

"I could look over the kids and say, 'Here are the many types of children I would never wish to raise.' My husband and I spent long hours talking about who we wanted our children to be: not their careers or who they would marry, but their hearts and souls. Their values—how they treated other people—that was the most important thing for me. My strong belief in firmness and consistency was an outgrowth of my experience as a teacher. I wouldn't have been as good a parent without that. Now that my kids are almost grown, it's the best feeling in the world to look at them and say, 'I like these people!' Even if I weren't their mother, I would *still* like them!"

For a caring parent, the best motivation for saying no is realizing it's the right thing to do for your kids. But there's an especially lovely bonus for you, too. Saying no *will* make your life easier in the long run. That's because children who learn to accept reasonable limits are a lot more pleasant to live with on a daily basis. When they know what you stand for—and what you won't stand for—they'll give up trying to wear you down by nagging, whining, and guilt-mongering. As a family, you will spend less time arguing and have more time to enjoy each other.

## Say Yes as a Family: Make a Difference

. . . . . . . . . . . . . . . . . . . . . . . . . . . . . . . . . . . . . . . . . . . . . . . . . . . . .

Tired of saying no all the time? One of the most powerful ways to instill good values is through positive action. Taking part as a family in charitable or community projects helps reinforce qualities such as concern for others, kindness, cooperation, and helpfulness. That's the kind of behavior we'd all like to see more of, at home and in our society.

Working as a team to make a difference brings families closer together. Seek out opportunities for you and your children to put your beliefs into action. A program sponsored by your church or synagogue may be just the ticket.

Some other ideas to consider:

- Spend a Saturday working on a community-improvement project. Clean up a park or creek, plant bulbs in a public garden, pick up litter from the beach. Look for announcements in your local paper calling for volunteers.
- Sign up the family for a fund-raising walk or bike-a-thon.
- Take part in a food drive or volunteer to work at the food pantry sorting donations.
- Go to a soup kitchen and help serve the hungry.
- Teach kids to collect used clothing, books, and toys to donate regularly to a thrift store or community-services facility. Or plan an annual neighborhood garage sale with the kids, and donate the money to charity.
- Volunteer to do yard work for an elderly person—family members can pitch in mowing the lawn, raking leaves, or making minor repairs. Help out a friend or neighbor, or contact an organization that serves seniors for a referral.

Cap off your day of positive action with a family treat: Take everyone out for pizza or have a picnic in the backyard.

One wise mother told us, "It gets tough sometimes, but there's always a reward for making the effort. In our family, we don't have too many long, drawn-out scenes because my kids know that won't work. Life around our house is usually pretty congenial. When I say no, they may complain, but I think they respect me for it. Of course, they would never tell me that! But my instinct says they do."

It only follows that when children aren't behaving in ways that stress you out and frazzle your nerves, it's easier to appreciate their good qualities. When your household stops being a battleground, you can stop resenting your kids because they never listen to you. Teach kids the behavior you expect, apply consequences when you don't get it, and sooner or later you *will* get results. You'll also have the agreeable opportunity to praise them for being cooperative and responsible—reinforcing the positive values you've helped to instill by saying no.

Less fighting, more peace and harmony. *Yes!*

# Saying No to High-Maintenance People

7

*My father is such a worrywart. He hates that I live in
New York. He calls nearly every night to make sure I'm okay.
I suppose it's good that he cares so much about me; but
having to constantly reassure him is driving me crazy.*

*A woman I work with is a world-class narcissist. She's
always telling long, involved stories about herself. To be
polite, I try to seem interested. But she never so much as
asks me whether I've had a good weekend!*

*Ellen is my best friend, so I like inviting her to my dinner
parties. But when she drinks, she's very unpredictable.
Sometimes she makes a fool of herself and ruins the whole
evening.*

Relationships are like cars: They need regular maintenance in
order to function properly. And if you get one that requires too
much work, too often, you might wonder whether you've got
a lemon on your hands.

Being a friend means occasionally being called upon to
play the role of patient listener, cheerleader, psychotherapist,
or social worker. What distinguishes high-maintenance people
(HMPs) from everyone else is that they're *always* forcing you
to play one or more of these roles. They just seem to need more

attention, more reassurance, more of your time and energy—not just in a crisis, but on a regular basis. With them, the division is clear: They demand, you supply.

The HMPs in your life may range from garden-variety difficult to severely neurotic and troubled. They might be egotistical, rude, cranky, anxious, depressed, or even drug-dependent. But frankly, their problems are not our primary concern here. Our aim isn't to help them cope with the world—it's to help *you* cope with *them*. And of this we're certain: The key to dealing with HMPs is recognizing what you can control and what you can't.

While you can't change another's difficult personality, you do have a choice about how to respond to it. You can speak out against rudeness and disrespect, protest behavior you object to, and set ground rules for spending time together.

You cannot summon magic words that will drive away a friend's depression or force him to abandon self-destructive habits. But you can encourage a troubled loved one to seek professional help and, if necessary, create some distance so his problems don't overwhelm you. In extreme cases, you can choose to live your life without a difficult high-maintenance person who may be endangering your physical, mental, or emotional health.

High-maintenance people come in countless varieties. Usually they're good people who mean no harm, and they often cause a lot more trouble for themselves than they do for you. But unless you are careful to protect your boundaries, certain HMPs can stress you, drain you with their neediness, or darken your world with their negative outlook. They can affect your confidence, your mood, or your entire point of view.

It's very difficult to stay energized and optimistic when you're in close contact with someone whose behavior is not respectful or whose personal problems are overtaking your own life. Even when you're committed to helping them, HMPs can have more influence on you than you have on them. Before they drag you down too far, you can (and must!) say no to letting them control your life.

That very idea—that there is a "line in the sand" we must draw when dealing with others—touches on a subject we hear a lot about these days: codependency. In very simple terms, it refers to an inability to separate oneself from another's problems, such as (but not limited to) alcoholism. Because this book focuses on practical techniques for setting limits, the whys and wherefores of codependency are beyond our scope here. But we do recognize that in some situations, finding the strength to say no to a loved one may require more help than we can provide. If that's the case for you, we suggest looking into some of the many good books available on the subject (see the Recommended Reading list on page 239). Elsewhere in this chapter you'll find information about organizations that also provide valuable support.

However, you can successfully manage most of the HMPs in your life by employing the strategies you'll find right here. In the following pages we'll look at some familiar "challenging" personality types and offer advice for responding to their problem behavior, both verbally and through other means.

Theoretically, we suppose, you could eliminate HMPs from your life altogether by simply avoiding them. But that's not a very practical solution, especially if it means having to divorce your husband or stop speaking to your mother! HMPs are everywhere, and often they're people you like or even love. If they have a few troublesome traits, they probably have others you appreciate, too. By finding ways to keep their "bad behavior" from overwhelming you, it becomes easier to focus on what you do cherish about the relationship.

Then again, HMPs may be people you don't like at all but are forced to associate with at work or elsewhere. But whether high-maintenance people are in your life by circumstance or choice, the way you deal with them can minimize the negative effects they have on you. Adjusting your attitude can help, too.

Try playing a little mental game with yourself. First, think of an adjective describing what it is about a certain HMP that bugs you; for example, let's say your sister is very argumentative. Then find another, more complimentary word for that adjective and decide that from now on you're going to think of the HMP in this new, more flattering light. Voilà! Your argumentative sister is now a spirited debater. In the same way, you can decide that your meddlesome, busybody aunt is just showing her love and concern or that your husband's noisy, rambunctious friends are really a bunch of vivacious, fun-loving fellows.

Playing the substitute-adjective game doesn't mean you're denying problems or copping out. It's simply a technique for thinking about HMPs in a more affectionate way so you can better manage the stress they cause you. By regarding their worst traits more sympathetically, it becomes easier to appreciate HMPs and to remember that in most cases they do add something positive to your life—at the very least, a little color!

In addition, the suggestions that follow can help you redefine the parameters of a relationship with someone who demands, expects, or needs more than you can comfortably give.

## A High-Maintenance Portrait Gallery

When you read through these descriptions, keep in mind that "high-maintenance" is a subjective term. A set of behaviors that would offend or burden one person might not faze you at all. Ultimately, it's for *you* to decide who the HMPs are in your life and whether you have the inner resources to keep on "maintaining" them as you always have.

The verbal responses that follow cover a variety of moods and are loosely arranged from mild statements to the more directly confrontational. We recommend trying the milder ones first and working down the list as needed.

Later on, we'll look at other practical strategies for changing the circumstances of your relationship with the high-maintenance person.

## But Enough About You: The Narcissist

Have you ever noticed when talking to certain people that every topic of conversation seems to quickly boomerang right back to one subject—them?

Narcissists take a toll on you by demanding lots of time and attention and giving you little or no acknowledgment in return. When you're with them, you're reduced to nodding, smiling, and trying to get a word in edgewise. If you do manage to speak, there's a good chance that whatever you say will be either ignored entirely or used as a springboard for the narcissist's next self-serving monologue. Tell him you've been invited to a state dinner at the White House, and he'll tell you how he turned down a similar invitation last year because he had something more important to do.

At first, narcissists may strike you as quite charming. Because they talk about themselves in such a flattering light, you may actually believe they are as fascinating as they think they are. Eventually, though, the charm wears off, and all that self-aggrandizement becomes a real bore. At its worst, the narcissist's apparent lack of interest in you can leave you feeling deflated and small. Because he's not really listening, it hardly seems worth the effort of trying to make yourself heard.

We're not too interested in why the narcissist needs to tout himself all the time. Sure, he's probably insecure—who isn't?—but unless he's your own child, that shouldn't be your problem. The important thing is knowing how to put on the brakes so he doesn't roll right over you.

How do you say no to the narcissist's self-centered way of controlling every conversation? There are ways of letting him know that you want to share the floor.

Steer the conversation your way with a statement "announcing" that it's your turn to talk.

- *I have a funny story I want to tell you.*
- *Let me tell you what happened at work today.*
- *There's been a lot going on with me, too, lately, and I'd like to share it with you.*
- *What a week I've had. I really need to vent for a few minutes.*

Depending on the tone of voice and facial expression you assume, you can pitch the following statements as either a good-natured ribbing or a direct challenge. If you need to, use the "time-out" hand signal to stop the flow of chatter.

- *Let's change the conversation to something we can both talk about.*
- *I've already finished my lunch, and you haven't touched yours yet. Does this tell us something about who's doing most of the talking?*
- *Is it my turn to talk now?*

If the narcissist is a relative or close friend, you may want to confront the situation and share your feeling that the relationship is out of balance. While there is always the risk of provoking a negative reaction, you will minimize conflict by avoiding accusations such as "You're so selfish; you think only about yourself." Instead, keep the discussion focused on how *you* feel (neglected, shortchanged) and what you want (more attention, more consideration). Use phrases like "My perception is . . ." or "This is how I experience it . . ." or "I need to feel that you care more." By presenting your feelings as simple facts, you will make it difficult for the HMP to argue with you.

- *I'm frustrated. I feel like when I talk, you're not really listening. To be honest, I need more of your attention.*
- *You know, you've been talking for forty-five minutes and haven't even asked me how I am. I have to tell you that sometimes I can't help but think you're just not interested in me. I'd like to feel a better balance in our relationship.*
- *I want to be honest with you about something. I wish I*

*could feel that you cared about what I have to say, but I get the impression that you don't.*

In response to the above, the narcissist will most likely protest or become defensive. Simply restate your case as often as necessary.

- *I'm not accusing you of deliberately trying to hurt me or make me feel bad. I just want you to know how our relationship feels to me. If I saw more evidence that you cared about what's going on in my life, it would make a big difference.*

## Yak, Yak, Yak: The Big Talker

Big talkers will never use three words when three hundred will do.

Unlike narcissists, big talkers prattle on incessantly, not just about themselves but about *anything*. This isn't necessarily bad. In fact, big talkers are often very intelligent, interesting people. You just wish they'd stop for breath once in a while and give someone else a chance to speak.

The first two groups of statements given above for narcissists will also help you gain control of the conversation from a big talker. Here are a few other ideas:

### Saying No to Big Talkers

The least confrontational way is to end the conversation.

- *I'd love to stay and chat, but I've got to run.*
- *Boy, there's a lot to say on that subject. I wish I had time to hear more, but this is not a good time for me.*
- *I can't really listen now; my mind is on something I need to do right away.*

When trapped by a big talker at work, change the subject back to a current project as gracefully as possible. Refer to the deadline and your need to get cracking.

- *Ha ha, that's a funny story. . . . Oh, no, is it already*

*Wednesday? The strategic plan is due on Friday. I'd better*
*hustle if I'm going to have it ready in time.*
- *Have I answered your question? If so, please excuse me,*
  *because I need to get back to work.*

If the big talker is your boss, ask a work-related question
to get her mind off whatever else she's going on about.
Preferably ask something you really do want to know. If she's
going to talk, it might as well be about something useful!
- *You're right, mangoes have gotten expensive lately. . . . Hey,*
  *I've been meaning to ask you . . . can you recommend a*
  *good mailing house? I need to get the new catalog out to*
  *our customers this week and I'm not too happy with the*
  *outfit we've been using.*

### On the Phone and Wanting Off

A friend of ours complained recently about arriving home one
night to find seven messages on his answering machine—all
from his mother! No, it wasn't an emergency, just a series of
anecdotes and opinions she wanted to share with him. It illustrates perfectly why the answering machine is your best friend.

If there's a chatterbox in your life, here are some ways to
spend less time on the phone, thus minimizing the need to cut a
call short:
- Leave the answering machine on at busy times, quiet times, or
  all the time. Communicate information to others by calling
  and leaving messages for them when you're sure they won't be
  there.
- With someone you're close to and want to check in on regularly, schedule a customary phone date. Long-distance relatives often do this, but even if your mother lives down the
  street and you talk every day, it's a nice way to add some
  structure to your phone time. By setting aside a special time
  to talk, you'll feel less guilty about not talking at other times.
- Limit time spent on the phone by calling from your job or

having the other person call you there. It's easy to break away from the conversation because of work obligations.

- Limit the length of phone conversations by scheduling them for times you know will be finite, such as in the morning before you leave for work or when you have something on the stove that will need your attention soon. Then you'll have a prearranged reason to get off the phone.

Here's what to say to end the conversation:

- *I'm really distracted now with everything going on around here. Is anything wrong, or is this a "Hi, I love you" call? I love you, too! Let's talk tomorrow, then.*
- *I want to hear what happened, but this isn't a good time to talk. Can you call me tomorrow at work around lunchtime — say, twelve-thirty?*
- *Mom, I want to hear about your day, but I want to talk to you when I'm awake enough to give you my full attention. Can I call you first thing in the morning?*

## As I Was Saying: Interrupters

It's insulting to be interrupted when you're trying to make a point. Or is it? In her bestselling book *You Just Don't Understand*, Deborah Tannen, Ph.D., points out that geographic and ethnic differences influence the way people perceive interruptions in conversation. What a Midwesterner might consider rude, a Brooklynite regards as lively repartee. So next time someone cuts you off, try to cut her a little slack—it could be just a mini–culture clash and nothing personal. But even native New Yorkers like us have our limits. When someone steps on our words a little too aggressively—meaning, they're even pushier than we are—here's how we put them in their place:

- *Hold that thought—I'm not finished yet.*
- *Please let me finish what I have to say.* (When finished, give back the floor.) *Now, what was it you wanted to say?*

## Saying No to Late-Night Phone Calls

Certain HMPs can really test the limits of your patience by calling late at night in order to unburden their souls, analyze a problem in great detail, or berate you for some perceived wrong you have done. Something heavy is weighing on their minds, and they want to share it with you. Right now!

Labor-intensive phone calls are never fun, and even worse when you're groggy from sleep. Your mind is fuzzy, your defenses are down. The goal here is to extricate yourself from the conversation quickly before it becomes impossible to escape. To avoid getting stuck on the phone half the night, don't respond to any of the caller's specific remarks or accusations. Instead, insist that the conversation be postponed till a more appropriate time. This allows you to be better prepared and think about what you want to say. When the HMP catches you by surprise, buy time.

- *I want to talk to you about this, but now isn't the time. I'm too tired/You woke me out of a sound sleep. Let's talk about it tomorrow.*
- *I'm sorry you're upset, but you're not being fair to me by calling at this hour. I can't think straight. I need to sleep.*
- *We've been over this many times, and I don't want to go over it again—at least, not now.*

But the best method of coping with late-night phone calls is to avoid them altogether. Use preventive tactics: Turn off the ringer on your phone and turn on your answering machine. If the situation warrants, leave an outgoing message for the late-night caller: *Carla, if this is you again, I got your twelve messages and I'll call you back tomorrow after three.*

Pleasant dreams.

- *Excuse me, I'm trying to make a point.*
- *Hey, I thought it was my turn. Give me a chance to speak.*

To keep group meetings from dissolving into incomprehensible babble, consider adopting the Native American practice of the talking stick. (No special stick required; a pencil or fork will do.) At any given moment, only the person holding the stick may speak, forcing others to listen before jumping in. When each speaker is finished, the stick is passed on to someone else.

## Woe Is Them: Hypochondriacs and Hard-Luck Cases

You think *you've* got troubles? These folks have more—and they want to tell you all about them in excruciating detail.

It can be quite a strain to spend time around someone who is morbidly preoccupied with illness or his own seemingly endless tribulations. If someone like this is a big presence in your life, you know how demoralizing such company can be.

It's true that people *do* get sick, and bad things *do* happen to good people. As a compassionate person, you want to react sympathetically. But these HMPs burden you with so many problems that you begin to suspect them of causing (or at least, worsening) their own distress. You've noticed that your frail, delicate friend's endless physical symptoms never seem to amount to anything. Or that another friend is *always* playing the role of victim in episode after episode. You wonder, "How could so much bad luck strike one person so often?"

Whether or not hypochondriacs and hard-luck cases are consciously trying to manipulate you, the effect is the same: You're cornered into consoling, reassuring, and offering solutions. Perhaps you even feel obliged to lend them money, excuse them from work or other responsibilities, or cover for them in some way. Result: anger, disapproval, and, of course, guilt over your coldhearted lack of empathy for this poor, unfortunate creature!

Hypochondriacs and hard-luck cases are frustrating be- 185

cause you're never quite sure how to respond. They cry wolf so often that if something *were* truly wrong, you might not know it. Tune them out entirely and you risk neglecting them during a genuine crisis. When the HMP is someone you're close to and care about, that's a big risk.

The fact is, anyone can turn into an HMP at certain times. When you're worried about your health, if you've had an accident, if you're going through a personal or professional crisis, if you're anxious about something, you're probably going to lean on friends or family a little harder than usual for some extra TLC. Remember times you've felt that way, and imagine what an ordeal life must feel like for a hypochondriac or hard-luck case who is stuck in that anxious, unhappy state all the time. It can't be fun. It helps to recognize that no matter how frustrated, angry, or annoyed these HMPs make you, they probably feel a lot worse than you do.

Next time you find yourself listening to woeful tales of doubtful credibility, ask specific questions designed to get at the facts or other information that can help you assess things objectively ("What did the doctor say, exactly?" "Did you ask the bank personnel to explain why money seems to be missing from your account?"). Avoid commiserating, as this will only encourage the HMP to moan on.

As with other HMPs, it's a lost cause to try to "cure" a hypochondriac or set the world aright for a hard-luck case. Telling him, "It's all in your head" or "I think you go out looking for trouble," isn't likely to change his pessimistic viewpoint (and it could start a big fight). A more realistic goal is to communicate somehow that your tolerance for complaining is limited. Say no to tales of woe.

### Saying No to Hypochondriacs and Hard-Luck Cases
- Prevention: Never ask "How are you?" It's literally asking for trouble. Instead, open conversations with a complimentary remark, preferably about the person's clothing, hair, or home. (*Hi! The place looks great. Is that new?*) Ask questions to get

the HMP on an upbeat track, e.g., *Did you catch that new comedy on ABC last night? . . . What color are you going to paint your bedroom? . . . Have you planned your flower garden yet for next year? . . . What are you wearing to Grandma's birthday party?*

When the grumbling starts, don't take the bait. Acknowledge feelings quickly and change the subject.

- *Hmmm . . . I hope you feel better soon. Say, you'll never guess who I ran into the other day. . . .*
- *Ah, that's too bad. . . . I hope you'll be able to work that out. By the way, I've been meaning to ask you . . . where did you stay when you went to Disney World? We're thinking of taking the kids down over spring break.*

### Send Hypochondriacs Where They Belong

To say, "I don't want to hear about it," to hypochondriacs, challenge them to take their problem to a medical professional. Whether they agree to or not, you then have the right to say, "Let's talk about something else."

- *I'm sorry about that pain in your side, but as I've already said, I have no idea what it could be. Since I'm not a doctor, it would be pointless for me to speculate, and I don't think you should either. If you're really concerned about it, call your internist. Why don't you make the appointment right now?*

Sometimes the best response is a little teasing:

- *You sure seem to have a lot of ailments. I hope none of them are contagious!*
- *Those sinus problems sound like they might be fatal. Have you made your Last Will and Testament yet?*

### Refuse the Blues

When the complaints of a hard-luck case go on too long, try to change the mood of the conversation with some Pollyanna tactics.

- *I'm sorry your car is in the shop again. These things happen. But let's keep it in perspective. It's better than you being in the hospital, right?*
- *That's too bad about your wallet being stolen again. But look on the bright side. You weren't attacked or hurt. As long as you're okay, the money isn't important.*
- *I have a wacky idea. Let's talk about something happy!*
- *Hey, let's change the subject. Tell me something good that happened to you this week.*

## Grumble, Grumble: The Terminally Cranky

Much as we're big proponents of saying no, there are those who would give our favorite two-letter word a bad name. These thoroughly negative naysayers are always ready to tell you why A is no damn good, B isn't what it used to be, and C just plain stinks. Other recurring themes of the terminally cranky: It'll never work. You can't trust anybody. Life is hard, and then you die.

You get the idea. Not only do these folks have no trouble saying no, they wouldn't know a "yes" if it came up and gave them a big fat kiss.

We have personally dealt with *lots* of cranky people over the years and would like to share our favorite response to them: teasing (also known as sarcasm). Maybe it's a little nasty. But for coping with the truly cantankerous, it's often just the ticket. Give it a try: Next time the terminal crank starts to rant, flash him your brightest Miss America smile, throw your arms wide, and sing him a chorus of "You Are the Sunshine of My Life" by Stevie Wonder. Not only will it throw your ill-tempered friend off guard, it will make *you* feel better.

When you have to spend time among the sour and surly, humor is a wonderful, effective defense. It's a way of saying, "I refuse to share your negative outlook on everything!" and more fun than stooping to the crank's disagreeable level. He may be stuck with himself, but you're not. Don't let him get under your skin—say no to terminal cranks!

Here are a few sample dialogues to get you started:

YOU: *I was thinking of going to Hawaii for vacation next year.*

CRANK: *Hawaii? It's so expensive! It rains every day! And the food is terrible!*

YOU: *Yes, I've heard—Hawaii is hell on earth. Guess I'll just have to put up with the hardship!*

CABDRIVER: *Look at that moron! Stupid #$@! doesn't know how to signal?. . .* (grumble grumble) *. . . These damn potholes. You can blame our useless mayor for that!* (grumble grumble) *. . . This used to be a decent neighborhood, but not anymore* (grumble grumble) *. . .*

YOU (departing): *It's been very enjoyable riding with you, sir. Keep smiling!*

## High Anxiety: Chronic Worriers

There are people who stay calm in a crisis. Then there are those who remain in crisis, even when everything is calm.

If you spend much time with a chronic, high-maintenance worrier, you'll know exactly what we're talking about—and you'll know these aren't the most relaxing people to be around. You can get pretty worn out trying to comfort a worrier who's fundamentally incapable of not worrying.

One type of chronic worrier needs an awful lot of hand-holding and constant reassurance that she is not as unworthy, incompetent, or unlovable as she feels. Here you have the friend who's always apologizing for no reason, or the nervous co-worker who needs corroboration for every decision she makes, or maybe even an insecure spouse or partner who's terrified you're going to leave.

Another type of chronic worrier is convinced that if something *can* go wrong, it *will*. Like the hostess who fears there won't be enough food to go around at her dinner party and that no one will want to eat it anyway. Or like one overprotective husband we knew who discouraged his wife from learning to drive because "it's too dangerous."

Either way, chronic worriers are perpetually geared up for disaster, rejection, or both. They ask a lot of "what if" questions: What if it rains? What if Grandpa falls down the stairs when no one's home? What if I say the wrong thing? What if we get chased by a bear? Your role, when with them, is to be the consoler, the voice of sanity and reason. That's all well and good when you're feeling sane and reasonable. The problem is, prolonged contact with a high-maintenance worrier can drive you absolutely nuts. (By the way, that's how to recognize high-maintenance worriers: They're the ones who drive you nuts.)

As with other types of HMPs, the key to coping with a worrier is understanding that *you can't ever solve the problem.* You can offer solace and solutions till you're blue in the face, but remember that in the larger sense, it's not any particular situation that's causing the worrier's woes. What keeps her keyed up is her compulsive need to fixate and fret about something . . . anything. What a torment it must be to worry so much about every little thing and to be so anxious about what other people think.

Okay, we admit it. We worry a lot, too. Not all the time, and not about everything, but let's just say we've had our moments, and we'll bet that you have, too. To one degree or another, we all must find ways to manage our anxieties so they don't rule our lives, sap our courage, and keep us from taking reasonable risks. Out-of-control worries can stand in the way of pursuing your goals and dreams. That's why it's so beneficial to have strong, inspiring role models in your life: They help you find the strength to face down your own doubts and worries.

An overly fearful, anxious person can act as a negative role model if her obsessive worrying starts to affect the way you think. Unless you maintain a healthy emotional distance, fears that at first appeared silly and unfounded may start to make sense. Worrying can be contagious. It is possible to become so enmeshed in someone else's anxieties that you begin to adopt them as your own and allow them to limit your own view of life's possibilities. This is especially true if you've grown up with a fearful, overprotective parent or have some other close relationship with a very anxious person.

Part of the process of saying no to a high-maintenance worrier should include an inner resolve not to become one yourself. Appreciate your own strength and the fact that you have enough to share some with someone else. One rather timid friend told us he actually likes talking to nervous, insecure people because "it makes me feel superior, in a way." He sees it as a chance to forget his own anxieties for a while and focus on someone else's. Because they don't threaten him personally, he can offer comfort and objectivity and appreciate the capable feeling he gets from playing that role.

Keep your focus on showing support, diverting worriers' attention, or making them laugh at themselves. Don't try to address every little problem they toss in your lap, because you can't. And don't let them worry *you*.

### Say No to Taking On Other People's Worries

Having someone who worries about you isn't the worst thing in the world. It's nice to know someone cares whether you live or die or whether you get caught in the rain without your umbrella. But if other people's worrying threatens to interfere with the life you want to live, set up some clear boundaries. Express appreciation for their concern, but let them know you've got your own agenda.

- *I know you hate to fly and you don't trust the airlines or the air-traffic-control system. But that's your fear, not mine. And I'm not going to let it stop me from going where I want to go.*
- *You're absolutely right. There's probably going to be a lot of traffic, and it will be tough to park. And yes, they're*

*predicting snow for later tonight. But it doesn't faze me—*
*I've coped with worse problems in my life!*

- *I appreciate your worrying about me; it shows that you*
  *care. And I care for you, too. Still, I'm going to take trapeze*
  *lessons whether you want me to or not.*

### Tease Their Worries Away

- *Wow, you are truly a first-class worrier—a real master. I'd*
  *never even think to worry about that!*
- *Next time I have a problem, can I give it to you to worry*
  *about? You're so much better at worrying than I am!*
- *Let's make a deal. From now until the wedding, you let me*
  *do all the worrying. When you think of all these little de-*
  *tails, just write them down, and every few days you can give*
  *me a list. You promise not to worry out loud, and I'll*
  *promise not to scream at you.*

### "What If" Questions

A reasonable response to "what if" questions that seem mad-
deningly trivial is to simply answer them with the truth. By
calmly acknowledging that possibility, you're saying in effect,
"So what? Whatever happens, we'll cope." For example:

- *"What if it rains?"* We'll get wet.
- *"What if the car breaks down?"* We'll call AAA.
- *"What if the kids get scared camping outside in the tent?"*
  They'll come in the house.
- *"What if we get hungry on the road?"* We'll stop and eat
  somewhere.

### "I'm Such a Loser" and Other Pitiful Cries

Modesty is a charming trait—in moderation. People who
overdo it by continually putting themselves down can be
strangely infuriating. Once you weary of building them up,
you might be tempted to agree with their self-deprecating remarks. Try changing their tune by actually doing this, in a
light-hearted fashion.

- *Until you told me, I never realized you were such a loser. All along I was thinking you were a sweet, kind, intelligent person that I really enjoy being with. But I guess I was wrong—thanks for setting me straight!*
- *You know, it's true. Why would anyone want to be friends with a terrible, awful person like you?*
- *I can only think of one really stupid thing you've ever said. ("What's that?") Just now, when you called yourself stupid.*

### Extreme Fears

At the extreme end of the worry scale, serious anxieties or phobias can cause real suffering and make it difficult to function. If this seems to be the case with someone you care about, gently remind this person that help is available. Treatments for anxiety and panic disorders often combine medication and therapy and are very effective. (See the sidebar on page 199 for resource information.)

- *Aunt Jean, you worry so much that it's making me worry about you. I'm afraid that you're carrying around a lot of anxiety that's keeping you from being as happy as you could be. There are very good treatments available for anxiety these days. Would you consider looking into them?*
- *Mom, you haven't been out of the house in months. I'm very concerned about you. It can't be easy living like this . . . and what would happen in an emergency? We need to talk to someone about getting some help for you. If you're not comfortable talking to your doctor, I'll call her myself. Okay?*

## Overcome by Sadness: The Depressed

There comes a point at which a friend or loved one may require more "maintenance" than you can ever provide. If someone close to you is seriously depressed, you may jump through hoops and try all sorts of approaches—from making jokes to getting angry—to get her to "snap out of it." Unfortunately, it's not likely there is anything you can say to make it all better.

Being around depressed people can be very stressful and confusing. Without a doubt, their lethargy, irritability, and general sense of resignation qualifies them as high-maintenance people, especially if you've taken on responsibility for trying to cheer them up. Mixed in with your sympathy and concern for a depressed friend or loved one, you're likely to feel frustrated and resentful, too. For this reason, you may be tempted to avoid her—and then feel guilty for turning your back at a time when she needs your love and support most.

In close relationships, another person's depression can have a harmful effect on your own happiness and well-being. In their book *When Someone You Love Is Depressed*, Laura Epstein Rosen, Ph.D., and Xavier Francisco Amador, Ph.D., point out, "If your partner is depressed, your marriage is nine times more likely to end in divorce than if you were married to a non-depressed person. . . . The relatives of depressed people have also been found to suffer from increased worry, resentment, and exhaustion. In fact, people who live with a depressed person are more prone to depression themselves and have a higher risk for other emotional problems, such as anxiety and phobias."

No matter how much you love a depressed person, you must protect yourself from being pulled into the emotional pit along with her. Having a clear sense of yourself as a separate person is essential, and that includes knowing your limitations and acknowledging your own needs. As much as necessary, plan activities that will bring you pleasure and help to keep your perspective in balance. Having something to look forward to, such as dinner out with your husband in a good restaurant, can make it easier to cope with a depressed friend or relative. Taking good care of yourself leaves you in better shape to help someone else.

The best thing you can do for a depressed person (and

your relationship) is to encourage her to get help from a mental-health professional. Let her know that you care about her and want her to feel better again. You can also show support by helping her investigate the treatment options in your area. The good news is that depression is very treatable through medication, therapy, or a combination of the two.

Still, it's possible that your advice will not be accepted. In that case, take steps to help yourself if the depression is casting a shadow over your life or if you are troubled about what your role should be. Read about depression and learn the best ways to communicate with a depressed person. Contact a mental-health organization and ask about resources in your area that might offer support for friends and family members of depressed people. (See the sidebar on page 199 and the Recommended Reading list on page 239.)

When a person you care about is depressed and suffering, it may be hard to keep your own emotions at a safe distance from her intense sadness. Don't avoid a loved one in the grip of depression. Say no to letting her depression consume your life. Tell her:

- *It really pains me to see you this unhappy. I wish there was something I could do. Have you thought about talking to your doctor about how sad and listless you feel all the time? You might be suffering from depression, and if you are, there are things you can do about it.*
- *I love you/I care for you, but this is more than I can handle. I don't know what else I can say. I want you to get help.*
- *I don't know how to help you feel better. I don't have any magic solutions. But I do know that depression is very treatable. I'd like to help you find someone who can help you. Will you let me do that?*

## Overcoming Resistance

Some people still attach a stigma to the idea of psychological treatment. Others may act stoical, believing that admitting to depression would be a sign of weakness. Try to reassure them that their fears are unfounded.

- *Depression is really very common. Millions of people go through it. In this day and age, nobody thinks you're crazy if you're suffering from depression. And there's absolutely nothing wrong with talking to a doctor or a therapist about it.*
- *Psychiatrists and psychologists are just another kind of specialist, like a cardiologist. You take care of your body, don't you? Sometimes you need to take care of your emotions, too.*
- *If you had pneumonia, you'd take antibiotics, wouldn't you? Depression is another condition you can treat. Lots of people get help for it. Why suffer like this if you don't have to?*

## Altered States: Alcoholics and Drug Abusers

Relationships are challenging enough when all parties are clean and sober. But alcohol or drug abuse can transform anyone into a truly high-maintenance individual.

A woman we know, married to an alcoholic who often became embarrassingly drunk at parties and in public places, finally announced that she would never again be seen with him in a place where alcohol was being served. We'd like to report that this was the wake-up call her husband needed, but it wasn't. He continued to drink excessively. Her disapproval did not change him, nor did the knowledge that his drinking was causing her pain.

However, this woman did accomplish something important. By refusing to put herself in situations that inevitably result in her becoming upset and humiliated, she protected herself from some of the negative effects of his behavior. She saw a way to say no, and she acted on it.

We think this story illustrates very clearly the limits of anyone's power to "solve" another person's alcohol or drug problem. If his addiction bothers you, but not him, the problem is yours, not his. That's why saying no to alcoholics and drug abusers requires focusing on the aspects of your relationship over which *you* have control.

Specifically, you can establish ground rules for the way you interact with a substance abuser. Restrict your contact to alcohol-free situations whenever possible. Insist on a no-drugs policy when you're together. Set limits on the behavior you are willing to put up with. If his excesses are making life intolerable for you, cutting ties altogether might be preferable to the status quo. (We probably all know of marriages that have dissolved for alcohol-related reasons—and others that should have.)

When someone you care about is abusing alcohol or drugs, it's discouraging to realize that no matter how much you beg, scold, threaten, or try to bargain with her to stop, it has no effect on her behavior. You simply don't have the power to change someone who doesn't truly want to change. The only behavior you can change is *yours*.

That's not to say that expressing your feelings is a waste of time. Why shouldn't your alcoholic friend hear that you're appalled she drove home drunk the other night? Your pot-smoking brother *deserves* to know that the brilliant insights he expounds when he's high sound boring and stupid to everyone else. A "tough love" approach is perfectly appropriate, because an alcoholic or drug user needs to know that her behavior has consequences. Ultimately it can destroy her health, her relationships, her entire life. Whether she chooses to deny that fact or embrace it is up to her. In the meantime, you'll feel better that you took a stand against behavior you find objectionable.

Within close relationships, certain kinds of tough love can feel like the hardest thing in the world—for example, if it involves breaking up a marriage or evicting an adult child from the house. Faced with this kind of challenge, the resulting guilt may be so enormous that it traps you into inaction. We would advise anyone in this kind of situation to explore any of the organizations, such as Al-Anon, that offer support to friends and family members of alcoholics and drug abusers. (See the sidebar on page 199 and the Recommended Reading list on page 239.)

Say no to martyrdom. Say no to taking responsibility for problems over which you have no control. Say no to putting *your* life on hold while waiting for someone else to address *his* problem.

### Saying No to Someone Else's Drinking or Drug Problem

To set clear boundaries when another's drinking or drug use is making you uncomfortable, focus on how this behavior affects you. Use "I" language.

- *Hanging out in bars just isn't fun for me. I don't enjoy drinking the way you and your friends do, so I'm not going to join you.*
- *You don't realize how different you get when you've been drinking. I feel like I'm with someone I don't even know, and it makes me really uncomfortable. Since it's hard for you not to drink in the evening, I'd prefer to spend time with you during the day.*
- *Sorry. I'm not going out to dinner/the party/that event with you because I don't like the way the evening goes when you've been drinking. When you have a handle on your drinking problem, invite me again, but until then count me out.*
- *It's your business whether or not you want to smoke pot. But when you do, it's impossible to talk to you. Frankly, it makes you stupid. So if you're going to get high, I don't want to be around you.*
- *My house is a drug-free zone. I don't want drugs here. I'll have to ask you to leave.*

# Help a Loved One . . . Help Yourself

. . . . . . . . . . . . . . . . . . . . . . . . . . . . . . . . . . . . . . . . . . . . . . . . . . . . . . . .

The better informed you are, the more equipped you will be to help a friend or loved one overcome an emotional disorder or substance-abuse problem. But even if your help is not accepted, take action to help yourself. The Web sites of the organizations listed below are all excellent places to begin exploring the many resources available; most provide links to related sites. (If you don't have access to the Internet, sign on at your local library.)

### DEPRESSION AND ANXIETY

*National Institute of Mental Health (NIMH)*—www.nimh.nih.gov
Comprehensive site offering information on symptoms, diagnosis, and treatments for anxiety and depression. Lists national mental-health organizations providing referrals to mental-health professionals and support groups in your area. Describes many free NIMH brochures available on-line or through the NIMH Information Line, (800) 421-4211. A list of organizations providing treatment referrals will be included in the mailing.

*National Mental Health Association*—www.nmha.org
Provides information about the Campaign on Clinical Depression, including treatment and referrals. Or call (800) 228-1114.

*Anxiety Disorders Association of America (ADAA)*—www.adaa.org
Offers information on anxiety and panic disorders (including phobias, obsessive-compulsive disorder and post-traumatic stress disorder) plus advice for family members, a chat room, and a listing of self-help groups and ADAA professional therapists around the country. Phone: (301) 231-9350.

### ALCOHOLISM AND DRUG ABUSE

*Alcoholics Anonymous (AA)*—www.alcoholics-anonymous.org
*Al-Anon*—www.Al-Anon-Alateen.org
Whether or not your loved one is willing to attend AA meetings, you

can get support from Al-Anon, the sister group for those affected by the alcoholism of a family member or friend. To find a meeting in your area, check your local phone directory or call (888) 425-2666. For information and literature, call (757)563-1600.

*Co-Dependents Anonymous*—www.codependents.org
This twelve-step organization supports people who go to extreme lengths trying to take care of other people's problems. Comprehensive site includes literature to order and a U.S. meeting list. Or call (602) 277-7991.

*Another Empty Bottle*—www.alcoholismhelp.com
An excellent Web site for friends, family members, and alcoholics themselves.
Includes information, resources, a discussion area and chat rooms, personal stories, "just for kids" content, a weekly newsletter, and treatment information. Links to many informative sites.

*SMART Recovery*—smartrecovery.org
Traditional twelve-step programs like Alcoholics Anonymous are not the only option for substance abusers. This is one of several alternative groups that take a different philosophical approach, emphasizing self-reliance over powerlessness. It may be effective for people who have been reluctant to join a twelve-step program or whose previous experience was unsuccessful. Site includes general information, on-line meetings, publications, member stories, links, and a list of local chapters. Phone: (216) 292-0220.

## Cutting Down on People Maintenance: A Few Strategies

In the preceding pages we've offered suggestions that we hope will help you set boundaries when talking to the high-maintenance people in your life. Now let's look at some broader strategies that will help you become a truly skilled manager of HMPs. These include knowing how to avoid new ones, losing some of your current ones, and minimizing or improving contact with those who aren't going anywhere.

## Prevention

Keeping HMPs out of your life is a lot easier than putting up with them after they've settled in. With this goal in mind, don't overlook the basic technique of Prevention. If you're already overtaxed by HMPs, you *can* choose not to get involved with another one. This requires keeping your radar on so you can detect their approach. Be on the lookout for egomaniacs, cranks, people who talk nonstop about their problems, or whatever type of HMP really presses your buttons. When you sense one hovering nearby, lie low. In practical terms: Be in a big hurry when you bump into them on the street. Graciously turn down their invitations. Let your answering machine pick up their calls. At work, be too busy to stop and chat. Take evasive action! Don't be rude or cold about it; simply be unavailable.

Stopping HMPs at the borders of your life can save you time, trouble, and maybe even serious emotional pain down the line. Just as you can say no to lunch with an egotistical bore, you can also choose not to begin a romance with someone who clearly has an alcohol problem. Employing preventive strategies is the simplest, most comfortable, and most nonconfrontational way to say no to people who would sap your energy or add to your stress level.

The important thing about Prevention is not to get carried away with it. Sending out too strong a "back off" vibe will make you a pretty lonely person. Someone who seems potentially difficult in one respect may have other qualities that make him well worth knowing. Be honest with yourself about the limits of your own compassion and patience, but be selective about whom you keep at arm's length. As part of that selection process, it helps to consider which traits in others are especially tough for you to cope with or burn up your fuse very quickly. Do fearful, needy people really drain and exhaust you with their insecurities? Then focus on keeping your distance from those who fit that profile. It may sound heartless, but at this early stage it really isn't. There's much less to feel guilty about, because they don't yet play a significant role in your life.

You don't always have the option to say no to high-maintenance people. So when you do have it, use it.

## The Ultimate "No": "Breaking Up" with a High-Maintenance Person

You may conclude that it's time to end your relationship with a certain HMP who is having a negative impact on your life. When this happens, there are two choices: the passive (or coward's) way, or actively "breaking up" with your friend.

We're all for taking the passive, cowardly route when the opportunity presents itself. Many friendships come to a natural end when one of the two parties moves away, gets a new job, has a baby, or develops new interests that take her into a different sphere. Under these circumstances, keeping up the friendship requires a greater effort than before, so it follows that if you don't want the relationship to continue, you can choose not to make the effort. Consciously refrain from making active contact, and allow other priorities to make you less available for the HMP. You're not "officially" ending the relationship but allowing it to fizzle out on its own.

However, the passive approach might not be enough to sever ties with your HMP, in which case you will have to "break up" in a more direct way. While this is not a pleasant task, if the person has hurt you in some way, your own anger and resentment should strengthen your resolve to go through with it. One man we know, for example, decided to cut ties with a longtime female friend who constantly put him down and made jokes at his expense. He wrote her a letter and said, in effect, "I don't want you in my life anymore, because whenever we're together, you make me feel bad." She returned his letter without comment, and the two have not spoken since. Rather than feel guilty about it, he's delighted to have freed himself from a so-called friend who had verbally attacked him for years.

When someone habitually treats you badly, breaking up is the right thing to do. Whether you do it in person or by letter or e-mail, the best approach, once again, is to focus less on the behavior itself and more on how it affects *you*, e.g., *When I'm with you I feel like I'm not being heard. I feel unappreciated. Rather than enhancing my life, this friendship is making me feel worse. It's not working for me.* Unless you're looking for a long, drawn-out battle, don't give the person an extensive rundown of her character flaws or rehash every offense she ever committed against you. (See also the section on saying no to a long-term romantic partner on page 101. Even when romance isn't a factor, the ground rules for ending a relationship are similar.)

Say no to HMPs who chip away at your self-esteem. Give up trying in vain to win their approval. For motivation, think of the confidence you'll gain, as well as the time and energy you'll save—precious resources you can now devote to people and pursuits that nourish you.

## When the HMP Is Here to Stay: Tips for Coping

Some high-maintenance people are just part of your life and that's that. When contact with HMPs is a given, you must find a way to cope.

Very often, HMPs are difficult to be around because their energy level is either too high or too low for your comfort. At one extreme are dominant, overbearing people who require a lot of attention. At the other end of the spectrum are those who are very low-key, withdrawn, perhaps depressed. These folks can leave you straining hard to keep up the conversation (and your spirits).

It is possible to make your time together more bearable, even enjoyable, by changing the ways you interact with the HMP. The following coping strategies can help you regulate the energy level and introduce new elements into your relationship to ease some of the stress. When you read through them, think about how you can apply these tactics with the people who frustrate, anger, depress, annoy, or otherwise drive you up a wall.

### Communicate Differently

- An HMP is less likely to overwhelm you in writing than she would over the phone. Say no to her excesses by communicating more via e-mail. You need not respond to complaints, criticism, or anything else you'd prefer to ignore. Keep the tone upbeat by circulating funny stories and jokes. E-mail is especially appropriate for long-distance family and old friends (tell them you have to cut down on your phone bill), but also suitable for locals.
- Use snail mail. The post office works just fine if e-mail isn't available, and you can include interesting articles or cartoons you've clipped. Introducing outside topics is a good way to divert attention from personal problems.
- Limit phone time. See "On the Phone and Wanting Off" on page 182 for some practical tips on how to do this.

### Set Ground Rules

Insist on specific terms before you agree to see the HMP. For example:

- Put a moratorium on a topic you don't want to hear about. (*I'd love to have lunch with you, but you have to promise not to spend it complaining about your father. He's off the agenda, okay?*)
- Stay away from bars. If you're fed up with a friend's drinking problem, tell him you'll see him only under alcohol-free circumstances. Make plans to dine at a restaurant that doesn't serve liquor, or invite him to your home. Or stick to daytime

activities: Walk on the beach, visit a museum, play softball. The point is not to "cure" him (you can't), but to protect yourself from behavior that distresses you. Remember, ground rules are *rules*; if he drinks in your presence, he breaks them. Don't stick around for it.

## Create a Diversion

To experience a difficult personality in its purest, most intense form, spend time together one-on-one with nothing to do but talk. But to lessen the impact a little, try the following:

- Get physical. Working up a sweat is probably less grueling than those long, heavy discussions across a dinner table. Bring your high-maintenance friend along to an aerobics or yoga class. Ride bikes. Play tennis. Go bowling or Rollerblading. Take a dance lesson. Throw a Frisbee. Not only is physical activity good for the body and mind, it will give you something new and different to talk about. This is especially recommended for dealing with low-energy or mildly depressed people.

- Rely on outside stimulation. This could refer to any activity that gives you and the HMP something to focus on besides yourselves: cards or a board game, a movie or video, books on tape, a sports event, a visit to a museum or a guided tour—anything you can think of. Outside activities help a lot when you're spending time among people with whom you have nothing in common—your relatives, for example.

- Work on a project together. Another way of focusing your attention (and the HMP's) elsewhere is to work together toward a goal. With certain kinds of high-maintenance people, consider asking for help on something they excel at and you don't. If they're insecure and underconfident, this will give them a chance to feel proficient and in charge. If they're hopelessly egotistical, you'll feel less obliged to compete with them in this particular arena. Suggestions:

  — Plan a dinner party you can shop for and prepare together.

— Ask her to teach you something you'd like to learn (e.g., a musical instrument, a foreign language, a computer program, sewing, or knitting).

— Build a piece of furniture.

— Paint the house (or part of it).

— Lay out plans for a garden and cultivate it together.

— Do some minor redecorating (rearrange the furniture, shop for and hang new curtains, buy picture frames and hang pictures).

• Share your HMP with friends. Whatever it is about the high-maintenance person that makes it difficult for you to be around him, having other people on the scene can take off some of the pressure. A group will absorb the HMP's negative energy or spread the force of his personality a bit further so you don't end up with such a big dose of it. There's also the possibility that two HMPs will find each other and ride off into the sunset! (Warning: This idea could backfire if your HMP is overbearing, obnoxious, or somehow not fit to be seen in polite society. Use it for people who will blend in reasonably well and not overpower the entire proceedings.)

### Practice Living in the Moment

Train your mind not to anticipate aggravation from an HMP and not to dwell on it after you part. For example, say you have a standing date to visit your difficult, demanding mother once a week. If you spend the three preceding days dreading your next visit and the three days afterward telling your friends how exasperating she was, a few hours of stress can stretch into a full week's worth. Instead, spend the other six days focusing on things you enjoy. Be present for the here and now, and difficult times won't consume your life. (Most meditation techniques help you learn to live in the moment. See the Recommended Reading list on page 239 for some excellent books on the subject.)

## Above All, Stay Positive!

When it comes to the HMPs in your life, the most important maintenance of all is maintaining a positive frame of mind. Yes, they try your patience. But in most cases they're in your life for a reason. Think about that reason, and you're apt to find something to feel grateful for. Instead of brooding about the negatives, focus instead on why you value that person. Your mother wants to run your life? Think about how glad you are that she's alive and well. Your childhood friend always gets on your nerves? Think about your shared history and the fun you have reminiscing. Remind yourself of the many qualities you admire in your high-maintenance husband. Whoever it is, when you really look for something to treasure, you usually find it: a generous heart, a quick wit, strength, intelligence, an adventurous spirit. Even your nasty boss may have something to teach you.

Very few people are purely and thoroughly awful. But if you're stuck with some, say no to letting them rule your world. Use the advice in this chapter. And most of all, make space in your life for whatever gives you happiness and purpose. Surround yourself with people who make you feel good about yourself, support you in your dreams, and inspire you to live a full and vibrant life.

# 8  Everyday "No's" Worth Knowing

............................................................

*Have you ever purchased something you didn't want because you hated to disappoint the salesperson?*

*Have you ever paid a bill that was 50 percent higher than the estimate because you didn't want to make a fuss?*

*Do you hate to tell your hairdresser you don't like the way she cuts your hair?*

We'd like to commend your extraordinary sensitivity and regard for the feelings of others. Unfortunately, we can't do that. This is a book about saying no without guilt, remember? We're here to *protect* you from your extraordinary sensitivity (and maybe, in the process, to save you some money).

When you go through life determined to please everyone you meet, it follows that you will have to endure things and experiences that don't please *you* one bit. This applies to random, everyday encounters with strangers as much as it does to our closest relationships. For example, if you're unable to disagree with or say no to salespeople, professionals, and other service providers, you're a sitting duck for all sorts of indignities. Medical procedures that may not be necessary. Shoddy home renovations. Bad food in restaurants. Strange, ugly haircuts. Remain silent, and someone else gets to call the shots. That's a pretty raw deal when you're the one paying the bill.

This chapter explores saying no in a variety of commonplace circumstances, including commercial and professional transactions where some people may be hesitant to question an expert's advice or walk away without buying. In addition, we'll discuss ways to cope with some typical situations that may disturb your peace at home and in public—from confronting noisy neighbors to fending off intrusive junk mail and phone calls.

For the miscellaneous challenges of everyday life, these "no's" are well worth knowing.

## Challenging the Experts

We see them as authority figures. We like to think that their expertise makes them infallible. Too often we feel humbled, deferential, reluctant to challenge their superior knowledge. Yes, we're talking about doctors. We're also talking about auto mechanics, plumbers, electricians, hairdressers, decorators, contractors, and anybody else who knows more than we do about something. Hail the experts!

Much as you may rely on them to fix your body, your car, or your house, the experts are human, of course. They make mistakes. They have their own tastes and biases that don't always mesh with yours. Some may not have your best interest at heart. You, as a patient, client, or customer, have the right to ask questions and to reject their advice if you find it unnecessary, overpriced, or inadequate in any way. If you're afraid to express doubts or seek another opinion, you forfeit your most basic rights as a consumer. Protect those rights by cultivating the ability to say no to a pro when you need to.

Finding the resolve to do that comes from respecting your own comfort level. If you know when you are at ease, you will come to recognize faster and faster when something or someone makes you ill at ease. If you are determined to protect your comfort zone, you will find more motivation to say no to the people who threaten it.

## Saying No to Doctors and Other Medical Types

There's an old saying, "To a hammer, the whole world looks like a nail." So when a surgeon recommends surgery, an orthodontist advises orthodontia, and a chiropractor says you need weekly spinal adjustments, it's important to remember that they're all seeing things through their own particular lens. That doesn't mean their advice is necessarily wrong, but it might not be the best course of action for you, either.

Think of yourself as an active participant in your own health care. The doctor is your consultant, not your boss, and just about everything is open to discussion. Don't forget that you're a customer paying for a service.

The very day a friend of ours was diagnosed with a serious illness, his doctor (a surgeon) scheduled him for surgery a few weeks later. In the intervening period, Ron set out to learn as much as he could about his condition. He spent hours on the Internet reading articles and communicating with other patients. He located a leading specialist in the field, with whom he consulted. It soon became clear that having surgery right away was only one of the options open to him; another treatment had been shown to be helpful as well. Ron decided to tell his doctor to postpone the surgery so he could first undertake this treatment. He felt confident about his decision because it was based on credible, authoritative information and the opinions of other respected doctors. (We're happy to report that more than two years later, he's feeling great and his prognosis is excellent.)

The point is that, barring emergencies, you can always buy time to consider your options when medical treatment is recommended—whether it's surgery, another procedure, or a medication with troubling side effects. A second opinion, your own research, or both may point toward an alternative that saves you considerable pain, trouble, expense, and inconvenience. Then again it may not. But you'll never know unless you can speak up assertively to doctors and other health professionals.

Following are suggested ways to do that.

### Buying Time to Learn More

- *I feel I need to learn much more about this procedure before I agree to have it done. Do you have any literature about it, or can you recommend any recent articles?* (You can also do research at the library or on the Internet.)
- *I feel I need to talk to a few people who have been through this and learn more about it. Are there local support groups you know about? I'd like to find out more about them and then get back to you.*
- *Can you give me the names of the top research doctors in this field? I'd like to read about any articles, studies, or clinical trials they've produced.*

### Buying Time to "Wait and See"

- *Since you tell me this condition sometimes clears up with medication, I'd rather go that route and see how things progress. I'm not eager to undergo an invasive procedure if I don't absolutely have to.*

### Getting a Second Opinion

- *This is a lot to think about all at once. For my own peace of mind, I'd like to learn more about it and get a second opinion before I make a decision. I'll call you after I do that.* (If your doctor tries to recommend someone, take the reference but disregard it, especially if the other doctor is in the same practice group or the same hospital. Find someone completely independent and objective for your second consultation.)

### "Is This Really Necessary?" Maybe Not

- *Those procedures sound pretty unpleasant. They're also going to be expensive. Before I go to that extreme, is there*

*something simpler I could try that might make me feel bet-*
*ter—some kind of medication or a change in diet?*

- *I simply can't come in every three months to have my teeth*
  *cleaned. But I'll floss every day, I promise.*

### Saying No to Medications

When the condition being treated is not life-threatening, you
may decide that "the cure is worse than the disease." That's
your choice.

- *I see that one of the side effects of this allergy drug is*
  *seizures. Under the circumstances, I'd rather put up with my*
  *sneezing and watery eyes.*
- *The possible side effects of this drug have me worried. I un-*
  *derstand that the odds of getting them are slim, but I prefer*
  *not to take the risk.*

### Saying No to Cosmetic or Nonessential Work

- *I see what you mean—my front teeth are chipping away a*
  *bit. But the cosmetic work you're recommending is expen-*
  *sive, and my insurance won't cover much of it. It's not a*
  *big priority for me, so I'm going to pass for now.*

### Saying No to Outrageous Billing

We're all accustomed to the high cost of medical care, but
gouging is wrong, even when the gouger is an eminent physi-
cian. If your doctor charges the same amount for a five-minute
follow-up visit as he did for the initial one, you're well within
your rights to question it. Whether or not the money comes directly out of your pocket is irrelevant, because inflated medical
bills result in higher insurance premiums for everyone. Say no
to obvious medical rip-offs. Start by asking your doctor to justify the inflated bill.

- *I don't understand. This bill is as high as the last time, yet I*
  *was only here for a few minutes. Since everything seems to*
  *be healing well, you didn't really have to do anything. Is*
  *this bill correct?*

If you're not satisfied with the doctor's explanation, you have the right to register your dissatisfaction.

- *This doesn't seem fair. I think your fee for taking care of this mole should include the follow-up visit.*

### "Our Time Is Up": Saying No to Your Shrink

Years ago a friend of ours was in psychoanalytic therapy—the "couch" variety—attending sessions twice a week. After many months, she was feeling better and decided she was ready to cut back to a once-a-week schedule and, soon after, end the relationship altogether. She geared up her courage to broach the subject with her psychiatrist, but on the day she planned to do so, the doctor beat her to the punch. "There's something I've been meaning to talk to you about," he said. "How would you feel about coming in *three* times a week?"

Many people in therapy find it difficult to say "no more" once they've decided it's time to move on. They fear that the therapist will say they're not ready or accuse them of running away from problems. It's true that if you're in therapy and want to quit, your therapist may feel that your decision is premature. Then again she may not. You'll never know until you bring it up. You're there to talk about your feelings, so why hold back?

Ultimately, of course, the decision to leave is yours to make, and you are not obliged to extend the "termination" process any longer than you wish to. Nothing is mandatory. Remember that if you later decide you were too hasty, you can probably go back. Your therapist isn't going to say, "I told you so."

Just don't break the news by announcing at the end of a session, "By the way, I'm not coming anymore." It's a good idea to allow at least a couple of sessions for the two of you to discuss your decision and review the progress you've made. It's also simple courtesy to give the therapist some advance notice that you'll be leaving.

If you can't find the right words to launch your discussion, try one of the following:

- *I feel I've gotten as much out of this process as I can. I've been thinking I'd like to bring it to a close.*
- *Coming to see you has been very helpful. In fact, it's helped me so much that I don't feel the need to continue much longer.*
- *I just don't feel that I'm making much progress here. I've decided it would be better if I stop coming.*

### Saying No to "Going Steady" with Chiropractors and Others

Maybe he touches you in wonderful ways, but you still don't want to see him every week. If you'd rather not make the commitment, say no to chiropractors, massage therapists, or other practitioners who pressure you for regular visits.

- *I can well imagine the benefits of coming on a regular basis, but I'm afraid it's just not possible.*
- *I appreciate what you do for me, but my insurance doesn't cover these visits, so I have to be selective about making appointments.*
- *If my time and budget allowed, it would be lovely to get a weekly massage, but I just can't do it right now.*

## Saying No on Behalf of Your Car

This time the ailing patient isn't you; it's a three-thousand-pound hunk of metal and rubber. But buying time and getting a second opinion are good practices when it comes to cars, too, especially if you don't know much about transmissions or manifolds. At the very least, comparison shopping will show you whether your garage is charging a fair price. If you want to feel better about the money you're investing in your car, don't say yes automatically to estimates or recommended repairs or parts. As long as the thing still runs, there's no reason *you* can't stall a bit.

### Buying Time

- *Thanks for the estimate. I'm going to shop around a little, but I may call you back.*
- *I'm not sure it's worth putting that kind of money into this old clunker. I'm going to think about it and get back to you.*
- *You say I only have a few thousand miles left on those front tires? Okay, I'll drive it for those few thousand, and then I'll be back. But I'm not ready to replace them today.*

## "You Didn't Get the Job": Saying No After Interviewing or Getting Estimates

Before you hire someone to paint your house, renovate your kitchen, or care for your children, you'll probably meet with several candidates to discuss the job, your schedule, and your budget. For a baby-sitter especially, you'll want to make sure the person you choose has the right personality and temperament for your family. You'll check references and, for a renovation or painting contract, get several estimates.

Inevitably there will be one or more people who don't get the job, in which case it's only fair to inform them of your decision. Don't leave them hanging, as this may cause them to rearrange their schedules or pass up other opportunities in the meantime. This "no" goes down easier when you supply a reason for your decision, preferably a nonpersonal one such as cost or inconvenient schedules.

A tip for the timid: Call when you expect to get an answering machine, and leave your "no" in a message. Some suggestions follow.

### Contractors and Painters

- *Thanks for coming out to give me an estimate. I found someone else who can start the job sooner/finish the job faster. I appreciate your time, and I'll keep you in mind for the future.*

Contractors and painters have a vested interest in knowing how their rates compare to the competition, so if money was the determining factor, don't feel shy about telling them.

- *I got several bids, and yours was among the highest, so I'm going with someone else. Thanks again for your time.*

Some contractors justify their higher rates by claiming to provide better-quality work or better service—and it may be true. Nevertheless, budget may still be your biggest consideration.

- *I know that you do very fine work, and your prices reflect that. For this particular job, though, that's more than I need. It's more of a budget issue, so I'm going to go with a less expensive painter.*

### Baby-sitters and Nannies

When telling a candidate she didn't get the job, give her a reason and try to find something positive to say as well. If you would have no reservations about giving her name to other parents, let her know that.

- *I realized I needed someone with more flexibility in her schedule, so I've hired someone who can come in the mornings in case one of the kids gets sick. Are you available for fill-in work? If so, I can call you for that and give your name to some other parents. People around here are always looking for good baby-sitters.*
- *You're obviously wonderful with children, and your references were great, but I wouldn't be able to pay you what you're looking for. We've decided to go with a young woman who's more affordable. Thanks so much for meeting with us. With your experience, someone will be lucky to hire you.*
- *I've decided to hire someone who's got a lot more experience. My kids can be a real challenge sometimes, and I wanted someone who can handle them when they're acting up. But all of us really enjoyed meeting you, and I think*

*you'd be great for the right family. I'll keep my ears open and pass your name on if I hear about another situation.*

If you didn't like the candidate at all, would never recommend her, and couldn't bring yourself to say anything like the above, keep it simple.

- *I wanted to let you know I've filled the position. We found someone who seems perfect for our family. I appreciate the time you spent with us, and we wish you the best of luck.*

## Saying No to Home-Improvers

In her business, Patti's a tough negotiator who says no many times a day. So why did she cower when she had to tell her contractor he installed the wrong bathtub?

Anyone who has survived a home renovation knows how easily things can go wrong. Mistakes get made. Communication breaks down. You allow someone else to set the agenda because you think that person knows better than you do or simply because you're sick of making decisions. *(What color* grout *do I want? I don't know! Just pick something and stop asking me all these questions!)*

Home renovations require patience and vigilance. And unless you maintain a cordial relationship with your contractors for the duration, things can get very unpleasant. Cut down on problems by asking lots of questions up front and studying your contract carefully before signing it. After the work begins, you may still have to say no to the wrong bathtub, the wrong grout, or the wrong something. If you can't say it, you'll end up living with (and paying for) the results.

We're pleased to announce that after calling all her friends for advice and moral support, Patti finally faced her contractor and got the bathtub she wanted. Here's what she said, along with some other suggestions for saying no to contractors and decorators who don't share your dream-house vision:

- *I'm sorry, this is not what I asked for. It's only fair that you*   217 *take it out and install the one I chose, without charging for any additional labor.*

### Resisting Unnecessary Improvements

- *There's nothing wrong with the current dishwasher, so no, we don't want to replace it. We're quite happy with it.*
- *No, we don't need a new refrigerator. This remodeling is costing plenty without having to change just for the sake of change.*

### Changing Your Mind

What happens if you decide you really hate those new tiles that looked so good in the magazine? When renovations are under way, it's a matter of "speak now or forever hold your peace." You're perfectly free to change your mind as long as you're willing to pay for the extra labor and materials and put up with possible delays. You can ask outright how much more it will cost, but you might benefit by posing the question a little vaguely.

- *I know I chose these tiles, but I'm just not happy with the way they look now that they're installed. What would the consequences be if I asked you to take them down?*

Once you've determined the change is worth it, say so.

- *I think it's better to admit now that I made a mistake! If I don't have those tiles removed, it's going to bother me forever.*

### Saying No to the Stylish

A contractor or decorator may urge you to adopt a style you don't really like or discourage you from something you've had your heart set on. Don't be cowed into thinking that "the expert knows best." In matters of taste, *your* taste should prevail. Embolden yourself to say no by keeping a vision in your mind of the home you want to be living in after the experts have

packed up and left.

- *I know that it's very stylish, but I wouldn't be comfortable living with it.*
- *The way my family lives, the minimalist look just wouldn't be realistic.*
- *Maybe it's true that the sixties are coming back, but this orange-and-yellow shag carpet just isn't me. Guess I'm just a beige kind of gal.*
- *I never really thought about having sconces installed, and to be honest, I just don't like the idea. I'd rather not have them.*
- *I'm sorry you hate the zebra-print wallpaper, but I absolutely love it. It brings back wonderful memories of my safaris to Africa. It's because of this wallpaper that I decided to redecorate my house in the first place, so I've just got to use it.*

## Saying No to Your Hairdresser and Others Who Want to Make You Look Fabulous

Hairdressers are fun people—at least the ones we've known have been. Maybe it's something about working in a salon where different personalities come and go all day, telling stories and sharing opinions. Who knows? But our impression is, people who cut hair for a living tend to be free spirits. They like to have a good time and try new things. The question is, do you want to wear that new thing on *your* head?

Unless you like surprises, make sure *you* decide what happens to your hair. Prevention makes all the difference here. Discuss the cut you want *before* the scissors come out. To resist a suggestion you're not wild about, try one of these responses:

- *Maybe I would look sexy with a perm/coloring/streaking/ Mohawk, but I wouldn't be comfortable with it. It's just not me.*
- *I wish you could do my hair for me every morning. I always look great when I walk out of here! But that style is too*

*much work for me to keep up by myself. It takes forever with the blow dryer, and I just don't have time. I need a cut that's really low-maintenance . . . just wash and go.*

- *Everyone tells me I'm beautiful just the way I am, so why go looking for trouble? I want the same haircut you gave me last time.*

### Say No to Six Weeks of Bad-Hair Days

Okay, maybe André got carried away with the scissors or left the chemical solution on a little too long. It'll grow back eventually. But at those prices, you deserve better.

When a customer is truly unhappy with a haircut or treatment, any good hairstylist will try to make things right at no additional charge. So if you feel like crying when you look in the mirror, don't suffer in silence. Share the pain with your hairdresser. Be as specific as you can. The more clearly you communicate what you don't like, the easier it will be to fix the problem.

- *There's still too much around my face. I'd like you to thin it out more in the front.*
- *This color just isn't flattering on me. It's too brassy. Can you bring it closer to my natural shade?*
- *I'm not comfortable with such curly hair. Can you do something to relax the perm?*

If you realize you hate it after leaving the salon, call up and request a repair appointment.

- *I tried to like the cut, but it's just too shaggy for my taste. I want to come back and have you even it out a little more.*

Is your hairdresser a great visionary who feels free to disregard your wishes in the name of artistic freedom? If your hairstylist treats you like an inanimate object and refuses to listen, don't sit still. If possible, get up out of the chair and leave. Tell the artiste:

- *I don't think we're communicating here. This isn't working. I'm going to go.*

Then look for a new stylist who isn't such a prima donna.

### Saying No to "Products" at the Salon

Our definition of a good hairstylist is one who gives you a great cut, has a friendly personality, and doesn't try to sell you expensive hair-care products. If you get a sales pitch at the salon, a simple "No, thank you" should suffice. But if someone pressures you, resist.

- *I'm sure they're very good products, but I'm happy with what I'm using.*
- *Frankly, it seems very expensive. I just can't see spending that much for styling gel.*
- *I've gotten this far in life without ever using "Intensive Conditioning Formula with Revolutionary Emollients"... so I think I can continue without it. Thanks anyway.*

### Saying No to Beauty-Industry Sales Pressure

Recently, while walking through Bloomingdale's in New York, our friend Gail was approached by a saleswoman offering a free skin-care consultation. Gail politely declined. "Are you sure?" said the woman. "I can show you what you're doing wrong." Stunned by the woman's rudeness, Gail couldn't think fast enough to respond, "What I'm doing wrong is standing here talking to you." But maybe you can use that line.

If you want to know how imperfect you are, plenty of cosmetics salespeople, not to mention beauty magazines and zillions of advertising messages, will be happy to remind you. In fact, they'll point out flaws you never knew you had: Your lips are too narrow, your brows are too thick, your nose is too big . . . and that's just your face. Preying on the customer's insecurities is a tried-and-true selling tactic. Is it so surprising, then, that women especially have so many insecurities to prey upon? It seems that the more credence you give to all those messages from the beauty industry—the more invested you are in achieving the perfect face, the perfect hair, the perfect body—the worse you end up feeling. When your self-image is fragile, it's very difficult to say no to people who want to sell you cosmetics or "tell you what you're doing wrong."

We don't buy it, and you don't have to, either. Here's our beauty secret: Ignore the whole damn thing. Turn away. Stop listening. Preserve your self-esteem (and lots of money) by practicing the basic technique of Prevention. In practical terms, you can:

- Give up reading beauty and fashion magazines. It's really easy, and this alone will drastically cut down on the number of "you're not good enough" messages you take in. (Read a good book instead, and you'll be beautiful *and* smart.)
- Steer clear of "free makeovers." They're free only if you can resist the sales pressure, and cosmetics salespeople often apply that pressure by pointing out so-called flaws that need to be "corrected."
- Find a few products you like, and stick with them. If you enjoy experimenting with makeup and trying new looks, fine. But if you want to save money, time, and trouble, decide which beauty products are essential for you ("none" is an acceptable answer), and then be done with it. That way you can tune out those millions of other advertising messages knowing you're not in the market for anything else.
- Focus your energy on being healthy, and beauty will follow. The lifestyle practices that contribute to good health also make you look better: regular cardiovascular exercise, strength training, plenty of fresh fruits and vegetables as part of a low-fat diet, enough sleep, and regular stress management. Taking good care of yourself from the inside out is empowering. You'll feel stronger, more confident, and proud of yourself. When you've got that down, you can't help but be beautiful. And when you're comfortable the way you are, it's easier to say no to people who make you uncomfortable.

# More Commercial No-no's

The everyday experiences of dining out and shopping present us with numerous opportunities for saying no. And when opportunity knocks . . .

## At Restaurants: Many Happy Returns

Your willingness to send back unsatisfactory food in a restaurant is the classic "Are you assertive enough?" test. So of course you must master it. But you don't have to get imperious and huffy to prove you can handle yourself in a restaurant. (That's not your style anyway, is it?) In this situation, there's nothing wrong with acting sweet and demure when someone makes a mistake at your expense. In fact, it's quite an effective approach. Just smile at the waiter and state the indisputable facts without assigning blame. Chances are the problem will be corrected as soon as you point it out.

### Mixed-Up Orders and Other Surprises
- *I'm sorry, but I ordered the tofu burger . . . and this appears to be chicken à la king.*

When the food you get on the plate doesn't match what you read on the menu:
- *I'm sorry, but the menu said the stir-fry came with saffron rice. If I'm not mistaken, these are Spaghetti-Os.*

If they tell you (a little late) that they're out of tofu burgers or saffron rice, tell them sweetly (but emphatically):
- *Oh. In that case, I'd like to order something else, please. May I see the menu again?*

### Lousy Food
Waiters don't do the cooking, so you won't hurt their feelings if you tell them your food doesn't taste right. At the same time,

be gracious about it and don't act as if you hold them personally responsible. Regard the waiter as your ally and special li-
aison to the chef, and be as specific as possible about what you
want. For example:

- *Could you ask the chef to cook this a bit more?*
- *You know, this is very salty.* (Begin to lift plate and hand it
  back to waiter.) *Could you ask the chef if he can do something about that?*
- *I'm sorry, but these vegetables are overcooked and soggy.
  Could you ask the kitchen to make me another order, just
  lightly steamed this time? You know what I mean. . . .*
  (Make eye contact and nod to show you assume that the
  waiter shares your good taste.)

Are you still feeling shy and reluctant to "bother" the waiter?
Just remind yourself that you're a courteous and respectful customer who's going to leave a decent tip. That alone should put
you on the A-list of restaurant patrons. And don't forget to say:

- *Thank you so much, I really appreciate it. This is* much *better.*

### Say No to Bad Tables

Remember, you don't *have to* sit where they tell you. In restaurants as in real estate, it's location, location, location. She who
speaks up gets the table away from the drafty door, the
kitchen, and the smoking section. Before you settle for less,
look around. If there's a better table available, ask for it, or tell
them you'll wait for one. It's as simple as:

- *I'd prefer that table over there.*

Enjoy your dinner.

## In Stores: Money Talks, and You Can Walk

Big department stores are so impersonal that you wonder if
anyone besides the guy at the security monitor is even noticing
you. We much prefer to shop in small stores and try to support

independent, local businesses whenever we can. However, because these stores operate on a more personal scale, and because the salesperson is often the proprietor, the shopping experience can occasionally get a little uncomfortable for the guilt-prone.

Say you're in a boutique, and you've spent the past forty-five minutes trying on outfits. There's a lovely saleswoman who's been helping you find your size, making suggestions, and saying things like "That's a great color for you." But you're not sold. Nothing's really grabbing you. You want to walk out, but you feel guilty not buying anything from such a nice, helpful lady. How do you make a graceful escape without dropping a bundle on a suit you'll never wear?

Remember that businesspeople thrive by developing relationships with customers. So even if you don't make a purchase that day, the saleswoman will appreciate knowing that you liked her merchandise and plan to return. She will still see you as a potential customer, one who may buy something the next time or mention her store to friends.

No retailer expects to make a sale every time, so keep in mind that any guilt you feel about browsing without buying is self-imposed. Here are some things to say as you leave the store empty-handed.

### Saying No to Purchases

- *Nothing is really working for me today. But you have some beautiful things here. I'll be back.*
- *If you had the green one in my size, I would definitely take it. Maybe I'll be luckier next time I come in.*
- *I'm still not sure, and I don't want to take up more of your time. I'm going to think about it.*
- Prevention: Avoid nonbuyer's guilt by telling the proprietor when you enter the store: *I'm just browsing today.*

In stores where salespeople work on commission (if they tell you their names, they probably do) you might feel a simi-

lar pressure to buy when someone's been giving you a lot of attention. In this case, cut her loose while assuring her she'll get
credit for any purchase you make.

- *I'm really not sure, but I don't want to keep you from other
customers. If I do buy it, I'll mention your name at the cash
register.*

## Saying No to the Junk Invasion

Our lives are full of junk—and not just the junk we buy because we can't say no. A great deal of it arrives uninvited in the
form of junk mail and intrusive telemarketing phone calls.
These may seem like petty annoyances, but it's important—
and gratifying—to give junk a resounding "no." It's also very
easy. There's little interpersonal communication involved, no
one to disappoint, no moral dilemmas to wrestle with. And the
rewards are lovely.

In this book, when we talk about saying no in order to reclaim time and create more space in our lives, we're usually
referring to impositions and distractions that come from other
people. But that's not always the case. The physical clutter
that accumulates everywhere also can weigh you down and
slow you down, whether it's piles of mail or your own possessions.

By saying no to junk in its tangible forms, you simultane-
ously say yes to a simpler, more streamlined daily life. You'll
have less mess to cope with, fewer irritations, fewer things to
stumble over, more room in your drawers and closets. There's
less to put away, less to dust and worry about breaking. When
you have clean counter space to work on, you feel more peaceful and relaxed. Think how annoying it is when the reverse is
true, when you're always having to move things out of the way
or search all over for what you need.

Why not liberate yourself by making a conscious decision
to get rid of superfluous stuff? If you haven't worn it or used

it in two years, you probably never will again. Donate it to an organization, give it away to friends (young people setting up their first homes make great recipients), have a garage sale, or sell it at a flea market or even through an on-line auction. And for the future:

- Adopt a "one-in, one-out" policy with items like clothing, books, videos, CDs, sports equipment, and other things that tend to multiply. When you buy something new, get rid of something old.

- Recognize that nothing is truly irreplaceable. There are so many *things* available out there—not just in stores but over the Internet, in libraries, and through friends—that if you do get rid of an item and then regret it, you probably won't have much trouble finding it or something pretty close again.

Letting go of your own junk isn't difficult when you focus on the space and serenity you'll gain from living an uncluttered life. Getting rid of uninvited junk is even easier.

## Junk Mail

If you've ever complained about slow mail delivery, consider that the nation's postal carriers haul about 4.5 million tons of third-class (junk) mail a year—almost 72 billion pieces, including promotional offers, catalogs, and solicitations. It's bound to slow them down a little. At the same time, junk mail costs U.S. taxpayers $450 million a year to dispose of—and requires 76.5 million trees to produce.

These eye-opening facts come from an invaluable booklet called "Stop Junk Mail Forever (Telemarketing & Spam, Too)," which provides comprehensive advice for getting your name off all kinds of mailing lists as well as warding off junk phone calls and e-mail. We strongly recommend this book to anyone who's serious about saying no to uninvited junk. (Order it by sending a check for $4.50 to Good Advice Press, Box 78, Elizaville, NY 12523.)

Junk mail adds clutter to your home and your life, and because each piece of it needs to be dealt with in one way or another, it wastes your time. When you consider that a good portion of it ends up in the trash without being opened or read, it seems like an even bigger waste.

But even if junk mail doesn't annoy you personally, it's worth resisting on behalf of the planet. Here are a few steps you can take that don't require much effort and can significantly cut down on the amount of junk that passes through your hands.

### Saying No to Junk Mail

- Write a postcard requesting that your name be removed from mailing lists. Send your name (include the different ways it appears on lists, e.g., Abigail Jones, Abby Jones, A. B. Jones, etc.), address, and signature to: Direct Marketing Association, Mail Preference Service, P.O. Box 9008, Farmingdale, NY 11735-9008. It won't eliminate all mailings but can reduce the amount you receive.
- If you've got a good credit rating, you probably receive tons of offers for "pre-approved" cards from banks and credit-card companies. One quick phone call can stem the tide of these mailings by removing your name from the marketing lists compiled by four major credit-reporting agencies. Call the Automated Opt-Out Request Line, (800) 353-0809.
- Every time you order anything via phone, mail, or on-line, request that your name not be sold, rented, or traded to any other outfit. If you do much ordering by mail, save time by having stickers made up with the words PLEASE DO NOT ADD, SELL, OR TRADE MY NAME TO ANY MAILING LISTS. THANK YOU. (These stickers are usually sold as return-address labels, but you can customize them any way you like. You may be able to order them through catalogs or packs of coupons you're already receiving.) Add a sticker to every order form and check you send. This goes for magazine subscriptions, campaign contributions, and charitable donations as well.
- If you like receiving certain catalogs but don't want your

name circulated further, ask that your name be kept on an "in-house only" list. (Send a note with your order, or call the company's 800 number.)

- Avoid responding to surveys, contests, or sweepstakes. Most likely your name will end up on yet another list.
- Think twice before returning warranty cards when you buy a new product. Their primary purpose isn't consumer protection—it's marketing. The personal information you supply (including your income and lifestyle interests) is added to a database and can then be sold to numerous direct marketers. You'll have the same warranty protection without returning the card, as long as you save your receipt. The only reason for returning warranty cards is so you can be notified if the product is recalled. For this, you need only supply your name, address, and the product's serial number.

### Say No Fast and Ruthlessly!

How often in life is it really okay to be ruthless? Here's your chance. Junk mail exists to be dealt with harshly. When it arrives, say no to opening it, reading it, thinking about it, and letting it pile up in your home. Sort your mail within reach of a trash can or recycling bin. If it's not first-class postage, dump it! The rule about junk mail: Don't touch it more than once. (If you feel guilty about dumping requests from charities, see page 27.)

## Telemarketers

Q: Why do telemarketers always call when you're in the middle of something important?

A: Because *anything* seems more important than talking to them.

Maybe there are people who don't mind dropping everything to listen to a stranger tell them by phone about some "exclusive opportunity" or "special limited-time offer," but we don't know any. As far as we can tell, telemarketers are a universal pet peeve, the most in-your-face form of junk selling. If you cherish the idea that your home is a sanctuary, a place where you have the right to live undisturbed by phone-generated sales pitches, say no to these intrusions.

Before we give you suggestions for doing that, we'd like to say a word on behalf of the folks who do the actual calling. Because junk phone calls are so widely despised, a lot of people feel no guilt at all about venting their anger at the individuals on the other end of the phone line. But after all, people who work in telemarketing are just trying to make a living. And it can't be easy, what with half the population telling them to jump in the lake (that's the censored version) and the boss looking over their shoulder "monitoring this call for quality assurance." At the very least, you've got to admire their courage. So be firm, but don't be unkind.

The key is to speak up quickly. Speed is of the essence when saying no to telemarketers, because once they start their spiel, you can get hooked, and before you know it, you're thinking, "Hmmm, sounds interesting . . . maybe I *will* subscribe to *Gopher Gazette*." Cutting the conversation short saves time for both of you.

Below are some ways to keep telemarketers from disturbing your peace, now and in the future. (For saying no to charitable solicitations, see page 30.)

### Anti-Telemarketing Tactics

- Prevention: Reduce the number of calls you get by requesting in writing that your name be removed from national telemarketing lists. Send your name, address, phone number, and signature on a postcard to: Direct Marketing Association, Telephone Preference Service, P.O. Box 9014, Farmingdale, NY 11735-9014.

Your request takes about ninety days to process, and your name stays on the "do not call" list for five years. It won't eliminate all the calls you get, but it's a good start.

### How to Hang Up on a Telemarketer

Whatever you do, don't respond to any specific points or questions from the caller (such as, "May I ask why you wouldn't be interested in saving up to fifty dollars on your long-distance service?"). A simple Policy statement, repeated if necessary, is all you need.

- *Sorry, it's my policy not to respond to phone solicitations.*
- *I don't do business over the phone.*
- *I'm sorry, but I have to cut you off. Nothing personal, but I don't take telemarketing calls.*

Most important, ask every marketer who calls to put your name on its "do not call" list. Once you ask, they are required by law to honor your request.

### What Doesn't Work in the Long Run

To avoid telemarketers, you might resort to such tactics as using your answering machine to screen calls, hanging up as soon as you realize it's a telemarketing call, or telling the caller that the person he's seeking (you, for example) isn't home. However, while these strategies offer temporary relief, they won't stop telemarketers from calling back again and again.

## Sticky Situations
...........................

When the neighbors play their stereo too loudly, they present you with a challenge. Do you confront them? Or do you swallow your anger, trying to convince yourself it's not *that* bad?

Life is full of awkward situations in which another person, possibly someone you don't even know, behaves in a way that disturbs you to a degree that's hard to ignore. These irritants can range from minor to highly obnoxious.

Taking the initiative and asking the offending party to stop is not an easy thing to do. People are unpredictable, and you can't always be sure the encounter will be a positive one. Yet, for quality-of-life reasons, we think it's well worth the effort it takes to face down your anxiety and make your feelings known. At best, you will solve the problem, and the disturbance will be eliminated. But even if you're not successful, you will get satisfaction from knowing that you took action. Speaking out relieves some of the pressure inside you and makes you feel like less of a victim. On the other hand, remaining silent just compounds your frustration: You're angry at the person who's disturbing you and at yourself for being unable to do anything about it.

Even though you can't control every situation to your liking, many times you do have the power to exert some influence. This section offers advice on how to communicate effectively with someone whose behavior is causing you stress.

## Neighborhood Annoyances

Your life could be perfect in every other way, but if your upstairs neighbors practice flamenco dancing every night from dusk till dawn, you're not going to be a happy person. It's the same with barking dogs, leaf blowers, lawn mowers, souped-up vehicles, and other forms of noise pollution. They keep you awake and disturb your peace. Don't blow a gasket. Be kind to yourself, and defend your comfort zone.

But how? You have to coexist on the same street or in the same building, so you'd like things to remain peaceful and friendly. Fine. That's exactly the right approach to take. When confronting a neighbor about a disturbance, give him the benefit of the doubt. It's possible he has no idea that he is disturbing you. Don't knock on his door geared up for a fight, or you'll probably get one. Instead, be cordial, ask politely, and expect cooperation.

### Confronting Neighbors

The following responses are given in two steps. With the first phrase, you inform your neighbor of the problem. Depending on his reaction, this may be enough—he'll apologize and promise to correct the situation. But if he doesn't immediately do that, you will need to be more direct. The phrases in parentheses, while still mild, take it one step further: They ask him to solve the problem. We've given examples, but you don't have to offer specific solutions. It's enough to say, "Can you do something about that?" When appropriate, try the "I'm sure you didn't realize this, but . . ." approach discussed on page 138.

- *You probably aren't aware how loud your stereo sounds in my apartment. (Would you mind keeping it lower?)*
- *You probably didn't realize this, but when you play your bagpipes, they sound very loud inside our house. (Can you practice somewhere else, or during daytime hours only?)*

Unless the person is deliberately rude or unreasonable, don't threaten to call the police or complain to your landlord or housing association—that's a deliberate provocation. Try first to negotiate a compromise as one human being to another.

- *The sound of your treadmill is pretty loud in my apartment downstairs. It makes all my dishes rattle. (Why don't we figure out the best times of day to use it so it won't be disturbing to me?)*

When the culprit is a canine:
- *Your dog is adorable, but I'm afraid he's been going on my lawn. I had to clean up after him twice last week. (Could you make sure he doesn't come visiting without you anymore?)*

### The Nonconfrontational Approach

One very mild technique is "playing dumb," i.e., acting as if you're not aware that the person you're speaking to is responsible for the disturbance. It may provide a strong enough hint to prevent future occurrences.

- *Did you hear all that racket last night? It sounded like Times Square on New Year's Eve! We were awake half the night—in fact, we almost called the police.*

Or maybe you suspect a neighbor's dog of leaving souvenirs on your lawn but have not actually witnessed it. Say to the dog's owner:

- *Have you noticed any stray dogs around the neighborhood lately? I've been finding poop on my front lawn, and there's damage to my grass. Have you been having the same problem?*

### Know Your Rights—Just in Case

As a backup, it's useful to know what your rights are. Does your community have leash laws regarding dogs? Does your condo require residents' floors to be covered by rugs to muffle sound? Citing the rules may be helpful in several ways: It makes your complaint seem more legitimate and a bit less personal, and it subtly reminds your neighbor that you have additional recourse if he is not cooperative.

- *I guess you weren't aware of this, but our neighborhood has an ordinance against lawn mowers before ten A.M. and after eight P.M.* (If your neighborhood doesn't have one, start talking to your neighbors and try to have one passed.)

### When All Else Fails

Formal complaints should be registered only as a last resort. But when your friendly attempts at problem-solving are unsuccessful, you may have to bring your case to a "higher authority." If you're up to the task, you could first try issuing a more forceful warning.

- *I've spoken to you before about the ordinance against lawn mowers in the early-morning hours. But this morning you were out again at seven A.M. I don't want to have to file a complaint against you, but if I have to, I will. Making noise at that hour is just not fair to me or the other neighbors.*

Nasty or just-plain-crazy neighbors *do* exist. Keep your distance from anyone who seems threatening or irrational.

## Won't You Be My Neighbor?

You may feel awkward asking your neighbor to correct a situation that's disturbing you. But the task will be a lot harder if the two of you have never even spoken before. It makes sense to cultivate good relations with your neighbors *before* any problems arise. Then, if one does come up, you'll have a context in which to discuss it. You're not just a stranger who appears out of nowhere to complain about something, you're a familiar, friendly face.

There are other reasons to establish a dialogue, even if it's just casual chitchat. For one thing, it's more fun to be social than solitary. And it makes the neighborhood safer, because you're more apt to keep an eye out for each other and notice if anything is amiss.

Inviting neighbors to an outdoor party or barbecue is a great way to make a connection with a lot of people at once. Or if you live in an apartment building, you might want to organize a get-to-know-you event in the lobby. If that's too much to take on, make an effort to attend other organized events that will put you in touch with neighbors, such as block parties or meetings of your neighborhood or condo association.

Reaching out in little, everyday ways makes a difference, too. Any modest gesture—a smile, a wave, and a comment about the weather—breaks the ice between you and another person. The small talk in itself isn't important, but making a connection is.

Becoming friendly with your neighbors makes all your encounters with them more pleasant—and the sticky ones will seem less intimidating.

## In-Transit Chitchat: Saying No to Fellow Travelers

You can meet plenty of interesting people en route from one place to another and have fascinating conversations with strangers who just happen to be sitting next to you on planes and trains. Getting to know someone new is a great way to pass the time when you're in a socializing frame of mind. However, you may have other priorities. Perhaps that transcontinental flight represents the only uninterrupted time you've had to yourself in weeks, and you were looking forward to reading a good book, listening to music, or getting some work done. You may really crave that solitude.

With most people, the obvious nonverbal cues—closing your eyes, sticking your nose in a book, putting on headphones, or pulling out a laptop—are enough to convey a "do not disturb" message. You can even wear earplugs to show you're not interested in talking. Giving very brief answers to questions, and not asking any yourself, also signals that you're not in a talkative mood. In a few cases, though, your chatty fellow traveler might be especially persistent and require you to end the conversation in a more obvious way. These phrases can help you gracefully stake out your private space.

### Reading
- *I'd love to chat, but I'm trying to get through this book before the end of the flight—I promised it to someone at the other end.*
- *I've been looking forward to unwinding with some magazines for weeks, but I've been so busy I haven't had the chance. I hope you'll excuse me.*

### Working
- *I hope you don't mind, but I'm on deadline with this project.*

- *Normally I'd love to talk, but I budgeted this time to catch up on my work.*

**Listening to Music**

Create a nice little cocoon for yourself by putting on headphones and closing your eyes.

- *I hope I don't seem antisocial, but I could use a little downtime.*
- *Please excuse me. I'm going to try to doze off for a while. Music helps me sleep.*

Little things mean a lot. Those everyday "no's" you say can make a big difference in how comfortable and happy you feel—in the world and inside your own skin. They give you the power to control the choices you make as a consumer, instead of paying for unwanted products and services or letting someone else's agenda prevail over your own. And they give you the power to restore peace when someone disturbs you, instead of suffering in pent-up silence. In countless ways, "no" puts power back in your hands.

. . .

We hope this book has given you the tools to say no more easily and with a greater sense of purpose. Keeping that purpose in sight, remembering and embracing what fulfills and delights you, is the best inspiration of all for saying no to the endless distractions and impositions that threaten to consume our days . . . and before we know it, our entire lives.

We know that by maintaining a strong vision of the "yeses" in your life, you'll find new resolve and confidence to say no without guilt. The beautiful irony of saying no to others is that ultimately it makes your relationships better, not worse. When you can invest your resources in your real passions and start living the life you want to live, you feel less frustrated, more joyful, and more generous. By reclaiming the time and space in your life to pursue your own priorities and dreams, you become more available, not less. Use the power that's rightfully yours. To the best life you can envision, say yes.

.   .   .

We'd love to hear from you. If you'd like to share an idea or story about saying no, please write to our e-mail address: notoguilt@aol.com

# Recommended Reading

..............................................

INSPIRATION FOR SAYING YES

Our favorite book for a new perspective on money, work, and personal satisfaction:
- Joe Dominguez and Vicki Robin. *Your Money or Your Life*. Viking Penguin, 1993

These books explore the ways we can create more ease and joy in our lives and realize our full potential:
- Carlson, Richard, Ph.D. *Don't Sweat the Small Stuff . . . and It's All Small Stuff*. Hyperion, 1997
- Fenchuk, Gary W. *Timeless Wisdom*. Cake Eaters Inc., 1998
- Gawain, Shakti. *Creative Visualization*. New World Library, 1995
- James, Jennifer, Ph.D. *Success Is the Quality of Your Journey* (revised and expanded edition). Newmarket Press, 1986
- Jeffers, Susan, Ph.D. *Feel the Fear and Do It Anyway*. Fawcett Columbine, 1987
- Keeffe, Carol. *How to Get What You Want in Life with the Money You Already Have*. Little, Brown, 1995
- Moran, Victoria. *Creating a Charmed Life*. Harper San Francisco, 1999
- Sloman, James. *Handbook for Humans*. OceanBlue Publishing, 1998
- Wieder, Marcia. *Doing Less and Having More*. William Morrow, 1998

For inspiration and practical ideas on slowing down, eliminating chaos, and creating a more spacious life:
- Benson, Herbert, M.D., with Miriam Z. Klipper. *The Relaxation Response*. Avon, 1990
- Carlson, Richard, and James Bailey. *Slowing Down to the Speed of Life*. Harper San Francisco, 1997.

- Easwaran, Eknath. *Meditation.* Nilgiri Press, 1991
  ———. *Take Your Time.* Nilgiri Press, 1994
- Luhrs, Janet. *The Simple Living Guide.* Broadway Books, 1997
- Menzel, Peter. *Material World.* Sierra Club Books, 1994
- St. James, Elaine. *Inner Simplicity.* Hyperion, 1995
  ———. *Living the Simple Life.* Hyperion, 1996
  ———. *Simplify Your Life.* Hyperion, 1994

## COMMUNICATING

For insight and advice on communicating successfully with family, friends, co-workers, and others:

- Horn, Sam. *Tongue Fu! How to Deflect, Disarm, and Defuse Any Verbal Conflict.* St. Martin's Press, 1996
- Martin, Judith. *Miss Manners' Basic Training: The Right Thing to Say.* Crown, 1998
- Tannen, Deborah, Ph.D. *Talking from Nine to Five.* Avon Books, 1995
  ———. *You Just Don't Understand: Women and Men in Conversation.* Ballantine, 1990

## MONEY

For inspiration and advice on financial abundance and philanthropic giving:

- Gary, Tracy, and Melissa Kohner. *Inspired Philanthropy.* Chardon Press, 1998
- Mogil, Christopher, and Anne Slepian with Peter Woodrow. *We Gave Away a Fortune.* New Society Publishers, 1992
- *More Than Money: Exploring the Personal, Political, and Spiritual Impact of Wealth in Our Lives* (quarterly newsletter of The Impact Project, a nonprofit organization assisting people with financial surplus to take charge of their money and their lives): The Impact Project, 21 Linwood St., Arlington, MA 02174.

## WORK

However you define career success, these books can help you achieve it:

- Carlson, Richard, Ph.D. *Don't Sweat the Small Stuff at Work.* Hyperion, 1998
  ———. *Don't Worry, Make Money.* Hyperion, 1997

- Chapman, Jack. *Negotiating Your Salary: How to Make $1,000 a Minute.* Ten Speed Press, 1996
- Faux, Marian. *Successful Free-lancing.* St. Martin's Press, 1983
- Lesonsky, Rieva, ed. *Entrepreneur Magazine's Start Your Own Business: The Only Start-up Book You'll Ever Need.* Entrepreneur Media Inc., 1998
- Steinberg, Leigh, with Michael D'Orso. *Winning with Integrity.* Villard, 1998
- Winter, Barbara J. *Making a Living Without a Job: Winning Ways for Creating Work That You Love.* Bantam, 1993

For help figuring out what sort of livelihood you want to say yes to:
- Bolles, Richard Nelson. *What Color Is Your Parachute?* Ten Speed Press, 1998
- Edwards, Paul and Sarah. *Finding Your Perfect Work.* Tarcher/Putnam, 1996

## DATING AND ROMANCE

For excellent advice in the realms of dating and relationships:
- Carlson, Richard, Ph.D., and Kris Carlson. *Don't Sweat the Small Stuff in Love.* Hyperion, 1999
- Gray, John. *Mars and Venus on a Date.* HarperCollins, 1997
- Kasl, Charlotte, Ph.D. *If the Buddha Dated.* Penguin Arkana, 1999
- Page, Susan. *If I'm So Wonderful, Why Am I Still Single?* Bantam Books, 1992
- Staheli, Lana, Ph.D. *"Affair-Proof" Your Marriage.* HarperCollins, 1997

## KIDS

We like these books for their expert, effective, user-friendly parenting advice:
- Carlson, Richard, Ph.D. *Don't Sweat the Small Stuff with Your Family.* Hyperion, 1998
- Carroll, Deborah. *Teaching Your Children Life Skills While Having a Life of Your Own.* Berkley Books, 1997
- Martin, Judith. *Miss Manners' Guide to Rearing Perfect Children.* Budget Book Service, 1997
- Samalin, Nancy, with Martha Moraghan Jablow. *Loving Your Child Is Not Enough: Positive Discipline That Works* (revised edition). Penguin, 1998
- Siegler, Ava L., Ph.D. *The Essential Guide to the New Adolescence: How to Raise an Emotionally Healthy Teenager.* Plume, 1998
- Taffel, Dr. Ron. *Parenting by Heart.* Addison-Wesley, 1991

### HIGH-MAINTENANCE PEOPLE

If you need help coping with difficult relationships, we recommend:

- Beattie, Melody. *Codependent No More.* Hazelden, 1992
- Forward, Susan, Ph.D., with Donna Frazier. *Emotional Blackmail: When the People in Your Life Use Fear, Obligation and Guilt to Manipulate You.* HarperCollins, 1998

  ———, with Craig Buck. *Toxic Parents: Overcoming Their Hurtful Legacy and Reclaiming Your Life.* Bantam, 1990
- Neuharth, Dan, Ph.D. *If You Had Controlling Parents.* HarperCollins, 1998
- Rosen, Laura Epstein, Ph.D., and Xavier Francisco Amador, Ph.D. *When Someone You Love Is Depressed.* Fireside, 1997

# Index